YORK NOTES

The Alchemist

Ben Jonson

Note by Chris Bailey

 Longman   York Press

Chris Balley is hereby identified as author of this work in accordance with Section 77 of the Copyright, Designs and Patents Act 1988

YORK PRESS
322 Old Brompton Road, London SW5 9JH

PEARSON EDUCATION LIMITED
Edinburgh Gate, Harlow,
Essex CM20 2JE, United Kingdom
Associated companies, branches and representatives throughout the world

First published 2000
Second impression 2007

ISBN: 978-0-582-42481-4

Designed by Vicki Pacey
Phototypeset by Gem Graphics, Trenance, Mawgan Porth, Cornwall
Colour reproduction and film output by Spectrum Colour
Produced by Pearson Education Asia Limited, Hong Kong

CONTENTS

PART ONE

INTRODUCTION

HOW TO STUDY A PLAY

Studying on your own requires self-discipline and a carefully thought-out work plan in order to be effective.

- Drama is a special kind of writing (the technical term is 'genre') because it needs a performance in the theatre to arrive at a full interpretation of its meaning. Try to imagine that you are a member of the audience when reading the play. Think about how it could be presented on the stage, not just about the words on the page.

- Drama is often about conflict of some sort (which may be below the surface). Identify the conflicts in the play and you will be close to identifying the large ideas or themes which bind all the parts together.

- Make careful notes on themes, character, plot and any subplots of the play.

- Why do you like or dislike the characters in the play? How do your feelings towards them develop and change?

- Playwrights find non-realistic ways of allowing an audience to see into the minds and motives of their characters, for example **soliloquy**, aside or music. Consider how such dramatic devices are used in the play.

- Think of the playwright writing the play. Why were these particular arrangements of events, characters and speeches chosen?

- Cite exact sources for all quotations, whether from the text itself or from critical commentaries. Wherever possible find your own examples from the play to back up your own opinions.

- Always express your ideas in your own words.

This York Note offers an introduction to *The Alchemist* and cannot substitute for close reading of the text and the study of secondary sources.

Ben Jonson's comedy *The Alchemist* has been almost continuously popular since its first performance in 1610. In the theatre it is apparent why this should be so: the pace is exhilarating, the wit is both sophisticated and rumbustious, and formidable learning is combined with elements of glorious farce.

But if you are encountering the play for the first time, the appeal can seem less obvious. What, for a start, is an alchemist? Alchemy was a pseudo-science which was practised chiefly in the Middle Ages but which was still flourishing in Jonson's time. The quest of the alchemist was to transform base metals such as lead into silver or gold. Modern chemical knowledge tells us that this is impossible, so what can the relevance of the play possibly be?

In fact, *The Alchemist* is not primarily about alchemy at all: it is about any sort of get-rich-quick scheme. Most people in Jonson's day knew that alchemy was a fraud, but that did not stop them *wanting* to believe that it might be genuine. A modern parallel might be astrology. Many people nowadays feel that astrology is an imposture, but that does not stop them from reading their horoscopes, and it is a similar double attitude towards alchemy that Jonson explores.

On stage, it swiftly becomes apparent to the audience that what Jonson's characters are practising is no more nor less than a con trick; that the alchemist, Subtle, is a fraud who simply *sounds* as if he knows what he is talking about. Subtle and his two accomplices, Face and Dol Common, could be confidence tricksters or suspect salesmen involved in pushing any one of a number of modern products: second-hand cars, pensions and investments, or time-share holidays.

What get-rich-quick schemes need are customers – in the case of *The Alchemist*, these are a parade of hapless victims who appear at the door of Subtle's 'laboratory' wanting to believe that he can make them rich beyond their wildest hopes. The greed of these people blinds them to the obvious implausibility of this venture and the impossibility of its making them their fortunes; and if one needs evidence of a modern parallel or relevance, one has only to think of the millions of people who each week spend money they can ill afford to spare on lotteries or football pools in pursuing the dream of effortless affluence. In laughing at the foolishness and gullibility of Drugger, Dapper, Mammon, and Jonson's other victims, we may be laughing at ourselves.

Putting oneself in the position of the victims or gulls is a way of resolving another difficulty that modern readers often experience with the play, which is that of its language. As you read the play, do not fret if you feel that you are not quite keeping up with what is going on; the whole point may be that you are not meant to! Subtle, for example, is simply baffling his customer with pseudo-science when he says to Mammon (II.3.60–64):

> No, sir, of red. F is come over the helm too,
> I thank my Maker, in S. Mary's bath,
> And shows *lac virginis*. Blessed be heaven.
> I sent you of his faeces there, calcined.
> Out of that calx, I ha' won the salt of mercury.

Subtle has performed none of the operations that he describes, even if he did know exactly what he was talking about. Desperate not to be left out, Mammon asks hopefully, 'By pouring on your rectified water?' only to be triumphantly capped by Subtle: 'Yes, and reverberating in Athanor.' (It is worth noting that even if Subtle may not fully comprehend his own utterances Jonson had done his homework, and his use of alchemical terminology in the play is usually accurate.) The language glosses that are included in the scene summaries of this Note make no extended attempt to explain the alchemical terms; Jonson frequently intends such terms only to mislead, and the student who spends too long trying to master them and to come to a full technical understanding of a passage such as that given above, will amass a lot of pointless pedantry at the expense of understanding what is actually going on in the play. (For those who are interested, most editions of *The Alchemist* will contain the relevant information. This Note includes some general information on alchemy in the Critical History & Broader Perspectives section.)

Therefore the reader should not be alarmed about failing to understand a passage such as the above. The reader is being put in the same position as Mammon or any of the other dupes. Language is part of the whole apparatus of trickery and bamboozlement. A modern parallel is again provided by the use of language by such people as financial advisers, who may leave those who seek their assistance more confused than enlightened. Sometimes the reader must simply 'surf' the language in all its bewildering unpredictability and energy. There is greater variety to Jonson's language than the above discussion of alchemical terminology would suggest. He captures, in a way that even Shakespeare did not, the speech and the slang of the contemporary London criminal underworld, as a survey of the language information given for the first scene of the play will quickly reveal.

Jonson has in the past suffered from unfavourable comparison with his older contemporary Shakespeare. As you start exploring *The Alchemist*, think about the play in comparison to any of Shakespeare's comedies that you may know. The plot of a Shakespearean comedy such as *Twelfth Night* or *Much Ado About Nothing* will often be romantic; there may be dark notes, but the play will end in reconciliation and harmony. The audience will be encouraged to engage emotionally with the characters, who will share their innermost thoughts with us, encouraging our sympathy and understanding. By contrast, Jonson's comedies can seem cold and forbidding. The laughter that is being encouraged may be harsh and mocking rather than warm and affectionate. There is nothing about romantic love in *The Alchemist*. The characters may appear to lack an inner life, any sense of deep thought and motivation, and be simply reacting automatically to external stimuli. Try to assess your own reactions to the characters and situations that you encounter. Jonson's characters are, when all is said and done, criminals: are you actually being invited to approve of their wit and ingenuity? Should you not instead be feeling some sympathy for their victims? Think especially about the ending of the play – is this *justice*, as you understand the word?

PART TWO

SUMMARIES & COMMENTARIES

There are often textual variants and disputed passages in the works of many sixteenth and seventeenth century playwrights – including Shakespeare – because of the casual attitude towards the printing and preservation of plays at that time, but few such problems exist with Jonson; *The Alchemist* was included in the 1616 volume of Jonson's collected works, the publication of which was overseen by him and which is the basis of modern editions of the play. Nowadays, *The Alchemist* is readily available in paperback selections containing several of Jonson's plays, such as those edited by Michael Jamieson for Penguin, Gordon Campbell for Oxford University Press and Helen Ostovich for Longman. Single texts of the play are edited by Brian Woolland for Cambridge University Press and, that on which this Note is based, by Elizabeth Cook in the New Mermaid series, published by A & C Black.

SYNOPSIS

An outbreak of the plague in London has resulted in a gentleman, Lovewit, moving temporarily to the country, leaving his Blackfriars house under the sole charge of Jeremy, his butler. Jeremy takes the opportunity to use the house as a centre for fraudulent activities. He transforms himself into one 'Captain Face', and enlists the aid of Subtle, an alchemist, and Dol Common, a prostitute.

The play opens with a violent quarrel between Face and Subtle, concerning the division of the spoils of their intended enterprise. Dol's common sense resolves the argument; they must work together as a team if they are to succeed. Their first customer is Dapper, a lawyer's clerk who desires Subtle to use his supposed necromantic skills to summon a familiar spirit which will help Dapper in his gambling ambitions. The tricksters suggest to Dapper that he may win the favour of the 'Queen of Fairy', so long as he subjects himself to various humiliating rituals. The second client is Drugger, a naïve tobacconist, who is pathetically eager for the help of 'necromancy' in establishing a profitable business. A rich nobleman, Sir Epicure Mammon then arrives, expressing fantastic visions of the benefits both material and spiritual that procurement of the 'philosopher's stone' will bring to him. He is accompanied by Surly, who is a sceptic and a debunker of the whole pretence of alchemy.

Surly is unable to dissuade Mammon from the error of his ways. Mammon is impressed by an alchemical show that is put on for his benefit, and he promises to deliver materials to be transmuted into gold. He catches a glimpse of Dol, and desires her. Ananias the Anabaptist arrives; the Puritans are just as eager as Mammon to attain the 'philosopher's stone'. Subtle contrives to become angry with Ananias, and demands that he should return with a senior member of his sect. Drugger returns and is given ludicrous advice about setting up his shop; he also brings the news that a rich young widow (Dame Pliant) and her brother (Kastril) have arrived in London. Pliant needs the services of a clairvoyant, and Kastril desires instruction in gentlemanly quarrelling. Subtle can help both of them. Face and Subtle both set their hearts on obtaining the widow.

The Anabaptists return. They agree to pay for goods to be transmuted into gold; these are in fact Mammon's goods. Dapper returns and is promised that the Queen of Fairy will be with him soon. Drugger brings Kastril who, on being told that Subtle is a skilled match-maker, rushes off to fetch his sister. Drugger is given to understand that the appropriate payment might secure his marriage to the widow. Dapper is blindfolded and subjected to 'fairy' humiliations; but on the reappearance of Mammon, he has to be gagged and is hastily thrust into the privy. Mammon is introduced to Dol. He has been told that Dol is a nobleman's sister who has gone mad, but he is not put off, and pays her extravagant compliments. Kastril and his sister come again. Kastril is given a lesson in quarrelling, and the widow captivates both Face and Subtle. They quarrel over who is to have her.

Surly returns, disguised as a Spanish nobleman. Face and Subtle believe that the Spaniard speaks no English, and they insult him. They also believe that he has come for a woman, but Dol is elsewhere in the building, engaged with Mammon, so Face has the inspiration of using Dame Pliant. She is reluctant to become a Spanish countess, but is vigorously persuaded by her brother to go off with Surly. The tricksters need to get rid of Mammon. Dol contrives a fit and there is an 'explosion' from the 'laboratory'. In addition, the lady's furious 'brother' is hunting for Mammon, who leaves. Surly reveals his true identity to Dame Pliant and hopes that she will look on him favourably as a consequence. Surly reveals his true identity to Face and Subtle, and denounces them. In quick succession Kastril, Drugger and Ananias return, and are set on to Surly, who retreats. Drugger is told to go and find a Spanish costume if he is to have a chance of claiming the widow. Dol brings news that the master of the house has returned.

Lovewit interrogates the neighbours as to what has been going on during his absence. Face is now the plausible Jeremy again, and explains that there cannot have been any visitors to the house – he has kept it locked up because it has been visited by the plague. Surly, Mammon, Kastril and the Anabaptists return. There is a cry from the privy; Dapper has chewed through his gag. Jeremy can no longer maintain his fiction. He promises Lovewit that if he pardons him, he will help him to obtain a rich widow. Dapper meets the 'Queen of Fairy' and departs happily. Drugger delivers the Spanish costume and is sent to find a parson. Face tells Subtle and Dol that he has confessed to Lovewit, and that officers are on the way; Subtle and Dol have to flee, empty-handed.

The victims come back again. Lovewit has married the widow and has claimed Mammon's goods; Surly and Mammon depart disconsolately. The Anabaptists and Drugger are summarily dismissed. Kastril accepts his sister's marriage to Lovewit. Lovewit pays tribute to the ingenuity of his servant, and Face asks for the audience's forgiveness.

DEDICATIONS, ARGUMENT AND PROLOGUE

Most play scripts of Jonson's time were regarded as temporary and insubstantial things, with no life beyond the actual performance, but it is typical of Jonson that he regarded his texts as literature that was worthy of preservation, and so *The Alchemist* is prefaced by the sort of apparatus that would more commonly be found at the beginning of a substantial poem. Even the Latin epigraph is portentous, being translated as: 'To seek out the Muses' garland where no one has won it before.' The Muses were the classical goddesses of the performing arts. Jonson is suggesting that plays prior to his would not have been worthy of the Muses' approval. (An understanding of the dedicatory material is not essential to a full appreciation of the play.)

DEDICATION

To Lady Wroth, niece of Sir Philip Sidney. The Sidneys were a great family of the time. Jonson says that sacrifices cannot be assessed in terms of the size or value of the item sacrificed, but can only be valued by the devotion with which they are offered and the grace with which they are received. In the same way, it is Lady Wroth's approval of the present humble offering, the book, that will give it its value. She belongs to the Sidney family, so he feels assured that her judgement will be sound. The dedication is short, over-familiarity being considered a form of dishonesty and one of the faults of the present age.

> **in the sight of** compared with
> **This** the present dedication
> **faces** rascals; perhaps with a play on the name of one of the chief characters in the drama

TO THE READER

This is not included in all editions of the play. Jonson laments the present quality of what is put on stage: most consists of 'jigs and dances', and it is the unnaturalness of what is staged that engages the audiences, who allow the authors of such material to get away with it; there is no control; and too much rubbish is produced. Occasionally 'something that is good, and great' may appear, but this only goes to show up all the more the dreadfulness of the rest. Jonson recommends discrimination and moderation. It is the 'unskilful' who believe that coarse things are better than those which are refined, and that disorder is preferable to that which is 'composed'. Jonson is making an indirect plea for classical discipline and harmony in the art of drama.

> **understander** one who understands; but also a punning reference to those who stand beneath the level of the stage, in other words the 'groundlings'.

Jonson is mischievously suggesting that the poor spectators may be quicker
on the uptake than those who can afford to pay for seats
one that takest up someone who actually buys a play-text; Jonson is warning
that nowadays you are likely to be disappointed
professors those that practise it
vice of judgements i.e. of arriving at mistaken verdicts

THE ARGUMENT

This is a brisk outline of the plot, in acrostic form.

narrow practice small-time swindlings
flies familiar spirits
flat bawdry downright prostitution
stone the so-called philosopher's stone, an alchemical agent for turning
base metals into gold. There is probably a pun on 'stone' as contemporary
slang for 'testicle'

PROLOGUE

This is the one item of the prefatory material that would have been
included in a contemporary performance. It is spoken by one of the actors
on behalf of the whole company ('we'). The play will be drawn from
London life, and its aim is the correction of vices and follies. The
observers may see themselves in the vices so depicted; the playwright
hopes that the audience will take the correction in good heart, and not
feel personally criticised.

Fortune luck will have nothing to do with the success of the play; that is up
to the discrimination of the audience
still always
spleen peevishness
here i.e. in this theatre
see and not yet own observe, but not feel personally attacked

ACT I

SCENE 1 **Face and Subtle are quarrelling violently; Dol Common attempts to appease them. They are interrupted by the arrival of their first customer**

Face (the Housekeeper) and Subtle (the Alchemist) enter arguing violently. Their female accomplice, Dol Common, attempts to keep the peace. Face is wielding a sword, and Subtle threatens him with a phial of acid. Face is the caretaker of the house while his master, Lovewit, is in the country for fear of the plague, and Subtle mocks his transformation since the departure of his master from poor servant to stylishly dressed 'Captain'. Face responds by saying that he rescued Subtle from poverty and helped to set him up in Lovewit's house as an alchemist. Subtle retaliates by claiming that not only did he raise Face in the world, but has transformed him so completely that his labour has been akin to a work of creation. It transpires that in Lovewit's absence the three have taken over the house in order to operate some sort of confidence trick. Face threatens to expose Subtle publicly as a fraud. In a lengthy outburst, Dol in her turn warns them that they will endanger their enterprise if they continue to fall out with each other. It becomes clear that the quarrel started because each of the men was claiming the greater share of the potential profits. Dol reminds the men of the punishments that they might suffer if their illegal operation is revealed. There is a ring at the door; it is a lawyer's clerk, Dapper, whom Face encountered the previous night and who is to be their first 'customer'.

> The first scene of *The Alchemist* is famously explosive in its impact. Not even the sleepiest member of the audience could fail to be alerted by Subtle's first line. Jonson's writing is very skilful, though, and he does much more than merely provide an energetic opening to the play. As the argument proceeds, the situation and the natures of the characters are explained and, crucially, Jonson establishes that the schemers do not trust each other. They are falling out even before their first victim has arrived. Their end is in their beginning.
>
> Face and Subtle accuse each other – somewhat ironically – of dishonesty and of putting on false appearances. Their insults are

exaggerated, but teach us much about their previous lives and their respective existences of drudgery and poverty. Face alleges that Subtle owes his present existence, with its potential for money-making, entirely to him; he gave Subtle credit, bought him his alchemical equipment and fuel, provided him with premises to operate from, and recruited his first 'customers' (lines 43–6). Previously, Subtle, says Face, had been close to starvation, living off 'steam … from cooks' stalls' (line 26), and had been dressed 'in the several rags' that he had 'picked from dunghills' (lines 33–4). Face gives his opinion of Subtle's intended alchemical operation and makes it clear from the outset, for the benefit of the audience, that the whole operation is a con trick. He refers to 'black arts' (line 46) and 'all thy tricks / Of coz'ning with a hollow coal' (lines 93–4), but it is also apparent that Subtle has other schemes in mind, and claims to be what Dapper is later to describe as a 'cunning-man', a supposed possessor of magical and arcane skills and knowledge. Face refers to Subtle's 'conjuring' (line 40), calls him a 'Witch' (line 107), and leads us to expect that Subtle's other talents will extend to divination: 'Searching for things lost, with a sieve, and shears'; astrology: 'Erecting figures, in your rows of houses'; and summoning spirits: 'Taking in of shadows, with a glass' (lines 95–7). It is in the hope of realising this last ability that Dapper arrives at the end of the scene; Face has told Dapper that Subtle will be able to conjure up a familiar spirit to help him with his gambling.

Subtle himself sounds as if he is beginning to believe his own publicity. He delivers an important speech in which he betrays signs of grandiosity and self-delusion, making claims for his 'own great art' (lines 64–80). He says that he has turned Face from a wretch whom 'no living thing / Would keep … company, but a spider, or worse' (lines 65–6) into a fashionable military gentleman with all the correct attributes of clothing, speech and social behaviour belonging to the sort of circle he is now to frequent; he has given Face 'Thy rules, to cheat at horse-race, cock-pit, cards, / Dice' (lines 75–6). It is a significant speech because it indicates to the audience that the notion of alchemy is not to be taken at face value, but as a metaphor for change and transformation in the play as a whole. Alchemical jargon is woven into the texture of Subtle's speech. Face, he claims, has been 'Sublimed', 'exalted', and 'Wrought ... to spirit'. Both transformations – that of base metal into fine through alchemy, and of Face from a menial into a gentleman – are false and superficial.

In another speech, Subtle is scornful of Face's assistance in providing him with the loan of Lovewit's house. Face, he alleges, was in desperate straits and would steal from his master, not being above profiting from the food and drink that Lovewit, as a gentleman, would have provided for the poor (lines 51–3). Face, like Subtle, would appear to be a man of many talents, and another operation that he allegedly ran was the supplying of gambling chips in reward for tips, which, says Subtle, made him 'some twenty marks' – over thirteen pounds, or more than four times his annual salary, if we are to believe the 'livery-three-pound' gibe of earlier in the scene (line 16).

The two are arguing about who rescued whom from poverty and is therefore entitled to the greater share of the eventual spoils. Face threatens to 'turn desperate' (line 88) and to expose Subtle as a fraud: 'in picture I will ... Write thee up bawd ... Told in red letters' (lines 91–8). This is a dangerous idea to entertain, and an ominous one for the audience to bear in mind. (Another ominous note is the mentioning of even the remote possibility of Lovewit's return: 'Pray heaven, / The master do not trouble us' (lines 180–1)). When Dol has calmed the two men down, Face still cannot resist a challenge: 'Prove today, who shall shark best' (line 160), a challenge to which Subtle consents. They are still playing one-upmanship; a different form of divisiveness. They have temporarily patched up their differences, but they are still not a team, whereas the theme of Dol herself is that of co-operation. She realises that in order to make a success of their venture – the 'venture tripartite' (line 135) – they must work as a unit.

'Doll' was one of many contemporary slang terms for a prostitute, and during the course of the play it is clear that Dol is happy to sell her favours, and also that both men hope to enjoy her, as when Face suggests that they draw straws to see which of them shall sleep with her that night, having her for his 'Dol Particular' (line 179). As the scene progresses, she is worried that the two men by their quarrelling will 'mar all' (line 81) by attracting the attention of their sanctimonious neighbours (line 164), who would not hesitate to report them to the authorities for engaging in illegal activities – Face has already spoken of the 'statute of sorcery' (line 112), an Act of Parliament passed in 1541 and again in 1604, forbidding all forms of witchcraft and conjuring, and he has also reminded Subtle of the danger of 'laundering gold and barbing it', or tampering with the coinage (line 114). Dol's theme in this first scene is that of 'All things in common' (line 135). They should all labour 'kindly' – like kin, or ones of a kind – 'in the common work' (line 156). She refers to Subtle as being the 'Sovereign' of the enterprise and to Face as its 'General'; she herself is 'Royal Dol' (line 174) and will later be a sort of parody 'Queen'. Dol describes herself as their 'republic' (line 110). Perhaps this indicates a dangerous confusion in the ordering of the enterprise, as a 'republic' would have no 'sovereign', but the contemporary audience would also pick up on the Latinate **pun** of the prostitute Dol being a *res publica*, or a 'public thing'.

The audience or reader should note the importance of the diversity and the forcefulness of the language in this first scene. Language is to be one of the key weapons of the tricksters as they adapt their tone and discourse to the situations they find themselves in and the people they find themselves with. Here, they signal their capacity for quick-thinking repartee and inventiveness, but the **imagery** of animals also signals a more ominous strain. Terms that occur include 'wild sheep', 'whelp', 'mongrel', 'Doctor Dog', 'scarab', 'vermin', 'dog-leech', 'brach', 'curs' and 'mastiff'. The contemporary belief was that it was the use of reason and the intellect that distinguished man from the beasts, and so for the three repeatedly to use such descriptions for each other strikes an unpromising note for the success of the undertaking; success will not be ensured unless Subtle and Face 'Fall to your couples again' (line 137) – a dog image this time used positively, as of a pair of hunting dogs working as a pair.

Dol urges that all three of them should 'Sustain our parts'. The idea of acting, of taking on roles and of changing appearances is also to be important to their project, and this is seen at the end of the scene when there is a call at the door. In the space of six lines a slick operation swings into action: Subtle goes to change into his conjuror's robes, Dol is instructed to hide herself – she is to be kept in reserve for this particular client – and Face puts on an act of departing, as though he were a mere acquaintance, and not an intimate of the Alchemist.

I will presumably, use the sword that he is later shown to have been brandishing

Thy worst do your worst!

I'll strip you that is, of your servant's costume

out of all your sleights stop your tricks

Sovereign, General Subtle and Face respectively

wild sheep blabbermouths

gum your silks spoil your fine clothes

strong water acid

and you come if you approach

suburb-captain bogus captain; someone preying on the criminal lifestyle for which the suburbs, the areas outside the City of London proper, were notorious

black and melancholic worms probably blackheads

advance your voice speak more loudly

algebra often associated with alchemy

linen underwear

make you tinder but to see a fire help you to start even a small fire

bawdry prostitution

buttery-hatch the kitchen door of a wealthy household, from where scraps of food (**chippings**) and beer might be distributed to the needy. Subtle is alleging that Face has kept the food and sold the beer

vails tips

credit to converse with cobwebs the means to be able to spend time in an empty house

your clothes spoken scornfully; your uniform has made you brave
fly out explode
houses signs of the zodiac
impostures ... printers the book will be so sensational that it will make as
much money for the printers as any alchemical operation could
a snarling dog-bolt a dog-bolt was a blunt-headed arrow that might stun but
was not often lethal; Dol perhaps means that the men are rowdy, but will
hurt no-one other than themselves
give betray
insult brag
claim a primacy, in the divisions lay claim to a major share of the
forthcoming profits
powder to project with in alchemy, the 'powder of projection' would be
thrown into a cauldron of base metal to supposedly transform it into a
precious metal – but Dol is speaking metaphorically of the ability to defraud
the dupes that all three of the 'venture tripartite' possess
sober, scurvy, precise neighbours in other words, Puritans
run themselves from breath make themselves breathless

SCENE 2   **The clerk Dapper arrives and is persauded to part with money in order to win the favour of the 'Queen of Fairy'**

Dapper, a lawyer's clerk, arrives to solicit the help of the 'Doctor'. He wants Subtle to raise him a familiar spirit that will assist his fortunes in gambling. Subtle puts on an act of appearing to be worried about the illegality of what he is being asked to do. Face urges Dapper's cause, then appears to lose his temper with Subtle. Subtle is swayed after money is offered, and then worries about the consequences of Dapper's achieving excessive wealth. Subtle 'knows' that Dapper is destined for great things because he is the sort of man who is loved by the Queen of Fairy. Dapper is given details of various ridiculous ceremonies that he must undertake in order to prepare himself for the arrival of the Queen. He is given a time for his return.

Face encountered Dapper at an inn the previous night; Subtle does not know Dapper at all. This is worth bearing in mind as we contemplate the brilliance of the double act that now swings into action. At the end of the first scene there was the most perfunctory allotting of roles: 'Seem you very reserved.' 'Enough' (I.1.197), and on the basis of this the two swindlers operate as if they have been working together for years.

Dapper's small-time pretensions are easily manipulated. He self-importantly claims to be without his watch – a status symbol it is unlikely he possesses – but his one overriding quality is his desperate eagerness to please. In his credulousness, he is easily taken in by Subtle's costume and by Face's insistence that the 'Doctor' is suffering moral scruples about what he is being asked to do, failing to appreciate the nonsense that a master of witchcraft should be fretting about legal niceties. He is desperate with anxiety as Face appears to fall out with Subtle, thinking that his hopes will be dashed, and he fails to appreciate the staginess of Subtle and Face's conversation about the Queen of Fairy, which is obviously intended for his ears. Face's mock outrage at his eavesdropping, followed by the imputation of untrustworthiness, destroys him completely, and leaves him wide open to the next stage of his humiliation, the preparations he must undergo for his meeting with the Queen of Fairy.

The tension in the relationship between Face and Subtle is skilfully maintained, as Face uses the pretext of falling out with the Doctor to carry on as he was in the first scene, in heaping abuse on Subtle. Yet the easiness with which they feed off each other's lines shows, as Dol had warned, that they need each other. Subtle awaits his moment before introducing the idea of the Queen of Fairy. Dapper insists that he is not 'allied' to the Queen, and Face's allegation of Dapper's unreliability (lines 131–5) results in Subtle's soothing 'No, no, he did but jest' (line 137); a smooth reversal of the situation at the beginning of the scene, when Face was pleading Dapper's cause against Subtle's apparent obduracy.

Another note of danger is sounded in the tendency of the two men to over-reach themselves, to do more than is necessary with their victims, just for the joy of it; this tendency will later result in some fatal complications. Here, besides Face's admiration of Dapper's fine qualities, we have his inventive portrayal of the Queen of Fairy as a rich and lonely lady who is longing for a partner to leave her riches to, and Subtle's description of Dapper's preparations (lines 165–70), in which the pseudo-necromancy contains the gestures of a Catholic making the sign of the cross and the sounds of Puritans at prayer. This is sheer unnecessary mischief. Jonson carefully plants the first indication of the time-scheme ('against one o'clock', line 164) that will be significant later.

pass-time timepiece

cunning-man possessor of magical knowledge or skill

halter noose

flies familiar spirits

velvet head this is Subtle's doctor's cap; it is made of velvet, so Face likens it to the 'velvet' or downy plush on a stag's antlers

embarked involved

humour must be law i.e. I consent to be swayed by the mood in which you make your decisions

rifling fly a minor spirit of gambling

great familiars powerful demons

Of forty worth forty

for him because of him

set him offered to him as a gambling proposition

ground foundation

o' the only best complexion the sort of character and temperament

to a cloak gallants would gamble with their expensive clothes; the cloak would be the last to go, as it concealed the loss of the rest

make him make him wealthy; make him a new man

allied related

caul o' your head the caul is the membrane enclosing the foetus before birth; it was the belief that if some of this attached itself to the head of a new-born child, then this was a good omen

ha't take it

compass understand

hap fortunately turn out

against ready for

twenty nobles a considerable amount of money. 'Her Grace's servants' will of course include Face

SCENE 3   The next customer to arrive is Abel Drugger, who wants
advice on how best to set up his tobacco shop

Abel Drugger runs a modest tobacconist's, and desires any necromantic
assistance that will enable his business to prosper. Subtle says that he
foresees a profitable future for Drugger, who has a horoscope that is
favourable for business. Subtle recommends changes to the appearance
and layout of the shop, and then hints that Drugger might be capable of
attaining the philosopher's stone, for which Drugger comically offers a
tiny amount of money. Face feels that he is getting the raw end of the
deal.

> Drugger, like Dapper, is so eager to have his desires fulfilled that
> he is easily hoodwinked. He immediately reveals his vulnerability –
> 'I am a young beginner' (line 7) – and his earnestness to please
> is indicated by the onward rush of his short phrases (lines 6–16),
> with his characteristic conjunction 'and'; in his nervous excitement,
> he cannot assemble a sustained and coherent statement. Subtle
> and Face treat him in a gentle and amused manner that is in
> pronounced contrast to their sudden urgency in the next scene,
> when the arrival of Mammon is announced.
>
> Face describes Drugger's business in a way that is ostensibly
> admiring, but he is also signalling to Subtle that he is well aware of
> all the opportunities for shady dealing that there are in the tobacco
> business – and Drugger does not practise these. Drugger is 'no
> gold-smith' (line 32) says Face, and Subtle picks up the message;
> Drugger is not a financial sophisticate. The whole approach of Face
> and Subtle is more domestic than it was with Dapper, where they
> played to his sexual fantasies. Drugger's desire is to run a tidy
> business of which he can be proud, and Face hints that the success
> that he would achieve through hiring their services would secure
> him the modest amounts of bourgeois status that he desires. When
> women are mentioned, it is as 'city-dames' (line 73) – good sources
> of business, with no further agenda such as Dapper appeared to be
> harbouring. Drugger is offered 'the philosopher's stone' (line 80)
> but hilariously misreads the offer. Throughout British theatrical
> history, distinguished actors have had success with the role of

Drugger; sometimes, in his helpless pathos, he scores unexpected victories, as his sheer naïveté poses problems that the sophisticated swindlers had never even thought of entertaining.

Drugger is to return later in the day, thereby establishing another subsequent twist in the plot. The scene concludes with a sudden note of bitterness from Face; Face is doing all of the footwork in seeking out clients, and is having to bear the day-to-day running costs, while Subtle sits inexpensively in the house. Once more, we have seen what a brilliant team Subtle and Face comprise, but there are tensions not far beneath the surface.

Good wives Subtle is pretending to address another group of clients
forbear be patient with
Troth in truth
Free of the Grocers no longer an apprentice, and admitted to the Grocers' guild; licensed to sell tobacco
art magical skills
sack-lees wine dregs
French beans the fragrant flowers of broad beans
no gold-smith he does not make gold; in other words, he does not charge extortionate prices for his tobacco
Already, sir, ha' you found it? Have you already divined the solution for him?
receipt recipe; formula or method
flies insects; or possibly malign spirits
boxes in which Drugger keeps his merchandise
directly with immediate success
crown about five shillings
portague a Portuguese coin, worth perhaps four pounds – still not enough, but worth having
stuff raw material, that is, the customers from whom to make a profit
veins the customers are compared to veins of precious metal in the earth, as sources of wealth

SCENE 4   **Dol announces the arrival of Sir Epicure Mammon**

Dol reports that Sir Epicure Mammon is approaching the house, and Subtle is immediately excited and orders Face and Dol to change their clothes. Sir Epicure is said to be already giving away his new riches in imagination.

Subtle no longer has time for his previous grotesque client ('your giantess, The bawd of Lambeth, lines 3–4) and his question when Dol reports the approach of their next visitor betrays a new excitement and urgency. Also new is the peremptory way in which he urges Face and Dol to change their costumes. His description of Mammon's gross behaviour is almost enthusiastic. If Mammon is excessive in his conduct, then Subtle's excitement at the prospect of his arrival betrays a similar weakness.

Mammon is described as being 'possessed' (line 16), behaving both as if mad and already in possession of untold riches. The 'philosopher's stone' was believed to be a universal agent of transmutation and, just as it changed base metals into gold, it was said to be able to make sick people healthy. There is a faintly blasphemous suggestion of Mammon walking amongst the sick like Christ. Subtle does not disagree with Mammon's reported belief that art (artifice, things made by man), although inferior to nature (God's creation), nonetheless can do more for mankind.

in a voice Dol disguises her voice

trunk speaking tube

Dispensing for the pox prescribing cures for syphilis

Reaching offering

spittle hospital at what is now Spital Square; then, a district notorious for prostitution

ACT II

SCENE 1   Mammon, accompanied by Surly, approaches the house

Mammon is trying to convince Surly of the wonders of alchemy, and Surly is extremely sceptical. Mammon has a vision of all the available metal turned into gold, and then he moves on to the medicinal effects of the philosopher's stone, or 'elixir'; it will be possible to reverse the ageing process, and all diseases will be curable. Mammon harks back to classical mythology and the earliest Biblical stories, adducing them all as evidence of the transforming powers of alchemy.

Mammon represents in extreme form the delusions that we have already seen more modestly and domestically in Dapper and Drugger. Mammon fantasises a world in which everything will be money; all of Surly's problems will be resolved as all the metal in his house is turned into gold. Mammon's vision expands. All the mines in England will become gold mines, and then he moves on to the medical benefits of the philosopher's stone, which will provide the key to health, long life, sexual potency and moral qualities such as 'honour ... respect' (line 50). As evidence for these possibilities, Mammon cites stories and passages from the Bible and from ancient legends, which have been interpreted as alchemical allegories.

Mammon is of course living in a dream world of complete self-delusion, but even as we want to laugh at him there is something so magnificently self-assured in the grandeur and totality of his vision that there may be a sneaking admiration for someone who can give himself up to an ideal, however absurd, so absolutely. Mammon personifies extreme greed, but one's reaction is complicated by the fact that he visualises solving many of the world's ills. His motives may indeed be self-serving, and the chief effect of his good works may be only to stroke his own personality, but there is something childlike and generous in his ideal of a world without disease, and promises such as ridding 'the plague / Out o' the kingdom, in three months' (lines 69–70) might have raised a yearning response in the contemporary audience.

Surly is an unlikely companion for Sir Epicure. He is sceptical in the extreme and assists the audience in voicing one natural reaction to some of Mammon's wilder fancies; but the reaction again is complicated, this time by the fact that Surly can claim no high moral ground. He is a cheating gamester ('the hollow die / Or the frail card', lines 9–10) and the difficult passage about 'keeping / The livery-punk' (lines 10–14) describes an extremely unsavoury contemporary practice known as a 'commodity swindle'. One may feel eventually that there is something too reductive and negative about Surly's unremitting joylessness.

be at charge have the expense

for the young heir to compromise a wealthy young man

seal sign a contract

in his shirt caught in a state of embarrassing undress

rude coarsely

viceroys a play on 'kings of vice'

great med'cine the philosopher's stone

piss a different golden rain

Marses plural of Mars, in Roman mythology the god of war. He was the father of Cupid

SCENE 2   **Mammon enters the house and continues describing his forthcoming life of luxury**

Mammon's descriptions this time are for the benefit of Face, now dressed as the bellows-operator, the alchemist's assistant. Mammon now reveals the true sensual excess of his appetites; all women and all foods shall be his. Surly reminds Mammon that the alchemist should be a man who is morally fit for his high duty, but Mammon has no doubt of Subtle's spiritual appropriateness.

Mammon continues in the same vein as in the previous scene, but now the true extent of his worldly desires is apparent. In the previous scene Mammon had spoken of unlimited wealth and of good works, but now he gets down to the precise detail of his hopes and desires, and there is nothing this time about helping other people. His cravings are drawn from the full extent of Jonson's reading in the more decadent corners of classical literature, and he draws himself up a menu of such excess that it directly recalls the depravity of similar feasts in the works of Roman writers such as Apicius and Petronius. The most extravagant and sensual poetry is given to the most gross, ridiculous and misguided character in the play; Jonson continues to disconcert and question the audience's expectations. As Mammon grows in monstrousness, the bloated magnificence of his debauched vision becomes ever more glorious.

Face plays his part to perfection, dressed as the Alchemist's wretched bellows-blower ('Lungs'). The complete professional, he is in sooty make-up too (line 19). He is able always to keep a straight 'face', and so when Mammon states that a requirement of the master of his harem is that he should be a castrato, Face meekly responds, 'Yes, sir' (line 34); we discover later from the designs that Face entertains of Dol that such a fate could not be further from his wishes. As the content of Mammon's speeches grows ever more immoderate, Face funnily feels a sudden urge to go to look after his fire. Surly is a largely passive figure in this scene, but at the end he reminds Mammon that the pursuit of the philosopher's stone has a spiritual aspect; the power to heal and to be able to create and to preserve life is not given freely and without moral responsibility. This reminds the audience of Subtle, and prepares them for his reappearance.

projection the final transmutation into gold

stuff metals to transmute

covering lead roofs

make me, a back create an ability for sexual performance

Hercules in the Greek legend, he made love with forty-nine of the fifty daughters of King Thespius in one night

blood, and spirit colour and purity

Tiberius ... Elephantis ... Aretine the Roman emperor Tiberius was reputed to have decorated a villa with pornographic pictures illustrating Greek poetry by Elephantis; similarly the Italian poet Aretino wrote erotic poems that were illustrated. Aretino is 'dull' in comparison to Mammon's fantasies

sublimed pure; but also an alchemical term

cuckold a man with an unfaithful wife

bawds go-betweens on sexual matters

divines clergymen

entertain retain

stallions sexual studs

belie deceive, betray

for them so far as they are concerned

beg ask to take charge of them

to make me eunuchs of I shall have them castrated

the spirit of Sol dissolved gold

Apicius Roman glutton and cookery writer

'gainst to prevent

carbuncle rounded gemstone

calvered cut up while still alive

Knots, godwits birds which would make exotic delicacies

beards fleshy threads around the mouth

how it heightens how the experiment is getting on

taffeta-sarsnet a fine silk

the Persian a reference to an ancient king of Nineveh who was fabled for his luxury; Mammon is saying that he will be able to excite this king to new excesses on seeing how Mammon rivals him

he must be *homo frugi* he must be a temperate man; Surly is aware that the man who achieves the philosopher's stone is supposed be pious and ascetic

That makes it, sir, he is so the man who does achieve the stone has these qualities, by definition

He, honest wretch Subtle!

for me as for me, so far as I am concerned

SCENE 3   In spite of Surly telling him the whole operation is a fraud, Mammon is completely won over by the supposed alchemical projects; he is also entranced by Dol

Subtle reminds Mammon that alchemical 'projection' can only be undertaken by those whose motives are pure, and Mammon assures him that this is the case. Subtle and Face, who is disguised, become the Alchemist and his assistant at work, complete with an impressive display of alchemical jargon. Surly can see that the whole operation is fraudulent, and delivers a sardonic commentary. Mammon is to bring all his goods of metal, for transmutation. Mammon is then given a glimpse of Dol and is instantly attracted to her. He is told that she is a lord's sister and has gone mad through reading too much Puritan theological writing. Mammon is advised that she is a beautiful and accomplished creature when in her right mind, and he is determined to pursue her. Surly is now certain that the house is a brothel. He receives a message, asking him to meet with Captain Face. This suits Surly's purposes, as he knows Face to be an infamous pimp who can perhaps help him to expose the true nature of what is going on at the house. He hints that he will return in disguise. Mammon urges Face to advance his cause with Dol.

In performance, it is customary in this scene to see Subtle and Face appropriately costumed, Subtle in impressive doctor's robes with a suggestion of the priestly, and Face in smoky rags. Face scurries in and out of an inner room or exit door, beyond which the supposed alchemical transformations are being conducted; modern productions often have fun with the sound of distant explosions and the release of clouds of colourful smoke. Even more important than any visual impact, though, is the language of this episode. We begin to see how language is itself an alchemical tool, something that can create change. Mammon actually *sees* nothing; the whole edifice of his aspirations is created by words.

Subtle opens with the smooth cadences and lulling rhythms of a prelate, as he cautions Mammon ('my son') to have the correct spiritual attitude to the good fortune he is about to enjoy. There is a rapid change in the pace as the two conspirators launch into their alchemical patter, which is punctuated by Surly's caustic asides. He can see what is going on, and he recognises the importance of the language in the performance: 'What a brave language here is? Next to canting?' (line 42). 'Canting' was the underworld slang or argot of thieves and beggars; Surly is recognising the purpose for which this new form of cant is intended. He engages Subtle in dispute, and the difference in rhythm between their two substantial speeches is marked. Subtle (lines 142–176) is still in priestly mode as he assembles a smooth and flowing argument in which he explains the principles of alchemy, while Surly (lines 183–198) spits scornful lists of the despised jargon: 'Your lato, azoch, zernich, chibrit, heautarit' (line 191). Surly realises that language is the source of Subtle's power, and it is language he uses to attack him. Surly, Face realises, 'has a parlous head' (line 315); his mind is cunning and he is dangerous to the enterprise, as he shows in this speech – he has an impressive alchemical vocabulary which he uses accurately. He knows what he is talking about, and Face is glad to get him off the premises.

The argument put forward by Subtle in his speech is that all things in nature aspire towards perfection. The philosopher's stone by which alchemists believed it was possible to transmute elements was regarded as an agent of perfection and power, and so it was felt to have a religious aspect. It was therefore necessary that those who aspired to the stone should demonstrate the appropriate goodness and wisdom; qualities which, of course, preclude any suggestion of greed or worldly motives – hence Subtle's priestly manner and Mammon's eager assertion of the 'pious uses' to which he will put his riches. It is not, of course, the intention of Subtle and Face that Mammon should gain any riches at all – instead, he is to bring them the contents of his own house. To this end they aim to tempt him into a sin that will compromise his supposed purity and lose him the stone – hence the introduction of Dol. The language of this scene becomes more and more explicitly sexual as it progresses, and it is apparent that the alchemical terms are also applicable to Mammon's mounting passions ('He's ripe for inceration: he stands warm', line 84) and to the dawning of Surly's realisation of what he feels is the true purpose of the business that is being transacted in the house. Surly tells Mammon to his face that he is being fleeced and that 'it is a bawdy-house' (line 298), but it is a sign of the intensity of Mammon's greed and of his lust for Dol that he completely ignores him and instead ingratiates himself with 'Lungs' whom he hopes will assist him to Dol's favours.

doubt suspect

I' the just point so punctually

worthy of a fear suggestive of a tendency

importune demands for instant gratification

e'en at approaching

Now grown a prodigy with now become so rare a habit amongst

particular personal

costive constipated; here, reluctant

register the next 170 lines contain a great deal of alchemical jargon, the purpose of which is solely to impress Mammon

covetise greed, a sin that would disqualify Mammon from receiving the philosopher's stone

crow's head ... cockscomb's the crow's head is a blue-black colour, one of the expected sequence of colours as described by Face at II.2.26; Surly suggests that a more appropriate description would be that of a cockscomb – the name of a sort of cap worn by professional fools

I looked for this I expected this

iterate the work repeat the process

in *potentia* potential

Materia liquida liquid matter

concorporate mixed together

ductile flexible

extensive capable of extension

charming bewitching

Sisyphus in Greek mythology, condemned to eternally roll a rock up a hill; a punishment for betraying the secrets of the gods

made ours common made our secrets known; Mammon assumes that Sisyphus must have revealed alchemical secrets

He'll be mad too – I warrant thee Face pretends to be frightened of Subtle's wrath; Mammon promises to protect him

mineral physic the application of chemical principles to medicine

Galen classical physician, here representing traditional medicine

This must not hear i.e. Surly

confederate banded together

She'll mount you ... oil Face compares Dol to an alchemical process, saying that she is as difficult to handle as quicksilver; there is a sexual suggestiveness in the language

vegetal lively person

of state about politics

wit 'whit' was sometimes used as a slang term for the female sexual organs

traduce defame

stone with a pun on the slang term for testicle

this bait Surly can see that Dol is part of the scheme to ensnare Mammon

original origin

And, this be if this is

the works the alchemical experiments

the party i.e. Dol

Marshal the provost-marshal, as at I.1.120

commodities i.e. prostitutes

Visitor official inspector
tire attire
a third person another reference to his proposed disguise
bite thine ear an expression of fondness!
make thee give you social prestige
bench ... chain perhaps to set Face up as a judge; ironic

SCENE 4   Subtle, Face and Dol are pleased with their success so far.
They prepare for the arrival of Ananias

Subtle and Face are confident that they have snared Mammon, and Face
sees no problems about dealing with such a threat as Surly may present.
A knock at the door announces the arrival of Ananias.

While the three tricksters move smoothly into their next positions,
tensions continue to simmer; Subtle patronises Dol and receives a
snappish response. A note of danger is sounded when Face appears
too dismissive of Surly. An intriguing extra dimension is added to
the story; it might be expected that somebody like Mammon would
want the philosopher's stone, but it appears that an austere Puritan
sect is also interested.

Lord Whats'hum's sister referring to the role Dol has played in the previous
scene
statelich in a stately manner; Subtle perhaps uses the Dutch word to
prepare us for the arrival of the Anabaptists, who in England were frequently
refugees from the Low Countries
race breeding
woman waiting woman, maidservant
gamester we are reminded of Surly's questionable background
that should deal Subtle is hoping to sell Mammon's kitchen equipment to
the Anabaptist!
exiled saints the Anabaptists were persecuted and therefore kept on the
move; 'saints' is sarcastic

SCENE 5   Ananias is treated contemptuously by Subtle

Subtle pretends not to know Ananias, deliberately misunderstands
him, and subjects him to a bewildering display of alchemical erudition.

Ananias refuses to advance more money, and is angrily dismissed by Subtle.

Jonson recognises that all strands of society share the same venial values, whether humble tradesmen like Drugger, depraved noblemen like Mammon or hypocritical self-styled deacons such as Ananias. Subtle has cynically commented at the end of the previous scene that he will employ 'a new tune, new gesture, but old language' (II.4.27), and he and Face put on a virtuoso display of alchemical cant for Ananias. Language is again their principal tool, but this time the approach is different; language was used to flatter and impress Mammon, but here it is used to browbeat Ananias. Ananias tries to assert linguistic superiority ('All's heathen, but the Hebrew', line 17) and he is instantly destroyed. His hypocrisies are easily exposed and there is something almost pitying in the way that Subtle plays along with his claim that the sect is dealing 'with widows' and with orphans' goods' (line 47). Subtle establishes that the sect is itself quite prepared to cheat and cozen. It becomes evident that Subtle has earlier taken the Anabaptist group for quite a ride, and he now has no compunction about contemptuously dismissing Ananias. He has calculated, quite accurately, that Ananias will bring his superiors to his assistance, and Subtle reckons that the bigger the fish to fry, the greater the potential rewards. However, as with the introduction of Dol into the Mammon plan, the schemers have perhaps once again over-reached themselves, and introduced an unnecessary complication into a scam that was running along quite nicely.

A Lullianist … artis Subtle deliberately misunderstands Ananias's statement that he is a 'brother' – that is, a Puritan – and instead quizzes him as to which sect of alchemists he belongs. Ananias is being subjected to a broadside of incomprehensible alchemical jargon
passion property
fugitive because of its volatility
pewter … ware the contents of Mammon's kitchen
the varlet that cozened the biblical Ananias defrauded his community
fright … appetite those raising objections must be given a fright, so that they come to their senses, and realise the benefits of the original arrangement

SCENE 6   Drugger returns, with news of the marriageable widow
           and her brother who wishes to learn the customs of a city
           gallant; Subtle can help in both departments

Drugger has reappeared, hoping for a cure for worms from the multi-
talented team (lines 82–4). He does not get this, but does get some
absurd advice about a lucky shop-sign for his business. He knows of
a rich young country widow who is eager to research her marriage
prospects, and her brother, a young gallant who is keen to learn of the
correct city customs of swaggering, quarrelling and generally throwing
one's weight about. Subtle can help in both cases. Drugger is persuaded
that the 'Doctor' may be able to advance his hopes with the young widow
but, once he has gone, Face and Subtle salaciously debate their own
prospects of laying hands on the lady. Dol must be kept in the dark
about this.

   'Faith, best let's see her first, and then determine' (line 91): another
   unresolved matter leaves an uneasy feeling at the end of this scene,
   and Subtle and Face are once more imprudently introducing extra
   complications into their schemes – but such is their magnificent
   confidence in their own abilities that the idea of difficulties never
   crosses their minds. They are happy to leave the issue of the lady in
   the air and, in spite of the vagueness of Drugger's information, each
   has decided, sight unseen, that the woman will be available for his
   own pleasure and that he is certain of success. They both expect to
   keep Dol for their own convenience, while entertaining the idea of
   dropping her without notice in favour of the new lady. Drugger's
   earnestness continues to win the audience's affection. Face's easy
   manipulation of him is enjoyable, but his tired contempt ('A
   miserable rogue,' line 81) leaves a sour taste – as does the distasteful
   sexual boasting at the end of the scene.

   A sign Drugger is keen to have a propitious shop sign devised
   constellation sign of the zodiac
   stale worn out, tired. Subtle claims to want to give Drugger something
   original, unique
   virtual powerful
   affections urges (for the merchandise)
   result upon have good results for

rug rough wool

anenst facing

legs acts of bowing

bona roba Latin for 'well dressed'; Face is asking, is she easy-going and sexually available? The term 'bona roba' was sometimes used as slang for 'prostitute'

up here i.e. to London

his match i.e. she is just as stupid as Drugger himself

blown abroad made public

Under a knight anyone less than a knight

water urine. If Drugger himself desires to marry the lady, then Face knows a 'Madam' who could use his urine to customise an irresistible love-potion for him

instrument set of instructions

for thee ... persuade Subtle may be able to make her look upon you favourably

damask rich silk

premises prospect

No offers no disagreement or haggling

parties the young lady and her brother

light promiscuous

grains a tiny unit of weight; the lady may be so morally light that she will need some weight added

endure her for the whole she could be such a trial that even her whole estate could not compensate a man for being married to her

ACT III

SCENE 1   **Ananias returns with Tribulation, who compares visiting an alchemist to entering Hell**

Subtle had evicted Ananias, instructing him to 'Send your Elders' at II.5.76, and so he now returns with his senior from the brotherhood. Tribulation reassures him that the 'chastisements' and 'rebukes' that he received are all a part of the trials sent to test the brethren. Ananias continues to express his unease about Subtle, and Tribulation explains that Subtle's heated behaviour comes from his working in proximity to fire, resulting in his being 'devilish'. He goes on to explain that the brethren's cause will be advanced if they can secure the philosopher's stone. Ananias now feels 'edified'.

Tribulation's sanctimoniousness and glib reasoning add another dimension to the gallery of questionable desires and motivations that the victims have demonstrated. Tribulation's arguments are specious in the extreme. He claims that Subtle's 'heat', his wrath, may profitably 'turn into a zeal' (line 31), enthusiasm for the Anabaptist cause. This leads him to assert that it is justifiable to desire the philosopher's stone so that the 'silenced Saints' (line 38), excommunicated Puritan clergy, can be restored to their rightful positions. He uses the phrase *aurum potabile*, 'drinkable gold' or, in alchemical terms, the elixir of life; but here, he is clearly referring to bribery which will persuade officials to become sympathetic to the Puritans: 'The only med'cine, for the civil magistrate, / T' incline him to a feeling of the cause' (lines 42–3). Tribulation's hypocrisy is clear. Expediency is all. It is quite acceptable to use illegal means if this results in power for the Anabaptists: 'We must bend unto all means' (line 11).

Saints how Tribulation sees the members of the Anabaptist sect
glassmen glass-blowers
Unto the motives the powers that influence
humours passions
weighing judging
Elder ... Scotland Puritanism was in the ascendancy in Scotland; Tribulation sees Scotland as an assurance of the eventual triumph of his sect
aurum potabile 'drinkable gold', or a cordial incorporating gold, used in medicine here, to dose or bribe the civil magistrate to make him sympathetic to the sect's cause
edified been strengthened by instruction

SCENE 2 **Subtle exploits Tribulation's greed, using extravagant promises to defraud him of more money**

Subtle affects anger, saying that the Puritans are only just in time and that his experiment has been nearly ruined. Tribulation is apologetic.

Subtle plays mercilessly on the Anabaptists' greed, intimating that he can advance their cause in a variety of ways. He goes on to provoke the Puritans, saying that they will no longer need to practise their customary pious frauds, but, in his eagerness to palliate him, Tribulation puts up with this, and swiftly stifles Ananias' occasional protests. Subtle promises the Puritans their reward within fifteen days. The object of Subtle's alchemical transmutation of base metal into gold is to be 'the orphans' goods' – in fact, Mammon's kitchen equipment, which he is planning to sell to the Anabaptists. With the gold, he will make 'good Dutch dollars', and, in his greed, Tribulation is quite prepared to overlook the illegality of a counterfeiting operation.

> The scene is full of comic potential. There is some lively by-play between the two Puritans. Ananias is the youthful and inexperienced zealot, who pounces upon doctrinally questionable words in Subtle's vocabulary (terms as innocent as 'Christmas', 'bell', 'idol', and even the date), but he is swiftly and amusingly quelled by the more political Tribulation, who has his eyes on a prize far greater than a short-term victory in a verbal quibble. Subtle plays with Tribulation skilfully and mercilessly. His big speech in lines 18 to 41 implies that, with sufficient gold, the Puritans would be able to finance a mercenary army supplied by a sympathetic power, and with 'the med'cinal use' they would be able to win the favours of powerful people. Subtle refers to the most outrageous illegalities, such as bribery and treachery against the state, with the promise of success for the supposedly pious brethren; he plays remorselessly on Tribulation's weakest point, his sense of his own righteousness, that allows him to blinker himself to any moral shortcomings. Tribulation is seen as an absolute hypocrite; for example, when he is tempted to state that 'We may be temporal lords' (line 52) – something that would be absolutely forbidden to an Anabaptist. He subsequently agrees to an act of forgery, accepting Subtle's distinction between 'coining' and 'casting' – counterfeiting and mere metal-working. In fact, both actions involved misrepresentation of the coinage and were therefore illegal, but Tribulation is able to turn a blind eye to anything which does not tie in with his own twisted motives.

ACT III

At the end of the play, Subtle is outwitted by Face, who shows himself to be the more adroit schemer and manipulator, but in the present scene we see Subtle at his finest. He reaches as far as he can without actually overbalancing. Having tempted Tribulation to dreams of military glory, which should have been completely outside the wholly spiritual area of Anabaptist desires, Subtle goes on to provoke and taunt him. Subtle promises unlimited riches, in order to suggest that the Anabaptists, after attainment of the philosopher's stone, will be able to rid themselves of many of the familiar patterns of typically extreme Puritan behaviour. He suggests that many Puritan customs and examples of their supposedly pious behaviour are mere fronts for monetary extortion (lines 69–96). He even suggests that the assumption of a name such as 'Tribulation' is an affectation, intended to 'catch the ear / Of the disciple' (lines 93–7), but in his eagerness to stay in favour with the Alchemist, Tribulation determinedly ignores all such insults, in the process revealing himself to be a greater hypocrite than we had yet imagined. Ananias might be made to appear a complete fool, but somehow he emerges with the greater dignity. Towards the end of the scene, Subtle is almost wearily scornful of Tribulation, knowing quite well that he will be able to persuade him that there will be no illegality involved in 'casting'. It is likely that Jonson himself had only recently renounced his own Catholicism, and his **satire** of the Puritans is vigorous and full-blooded.

threescore minutes as mentioned at II.5.84
it goes down yet it may yet be ruined, because of the presence of wicked Ananias
qualify reduce the offence
numbered provided
main principal purpose
Hollanders the Dutch were more sympathetic than most to the Anabaptist sect, and Subtle suggests that they might be bought as military allies, using the funds provided by the philosopher's stone
incombustible alchemically refined to resist fire
friends lovers
bone-ache venereal disease

Christ-tide the suggestion of 'mass' would carry popish suggestions

Long-winded exercises devotions

suck up swallow

ha, and hum mannerisms of Puritans at prayer

phlegmatic lethargic; hence, lacking Puritan zeal

tune hymn

it is your bell Subtle suggests that the Puritans should set their sermons as hymns, which might then be as effective as church bells in assembling a congregation. He is seeing how much offence Tribulation will endure without protest in his eagerness to obtain the stone

neither ... somewhere his zeal did not forbid there to be a hymn-tune sometimes; his attitude is the same as yours really

toward close to

we shall not need we shall not need hymns once we have the philosopher's stone

take ... one day seize the security on a loan that is only just overdue

Starch even this attracted Puritan censure; in shaping clothes, it was thought to be an instrument of worldly vanity

against the hearing so that you do not have to hear

wire-drawn grace lengthy prayer before a meal

custard served at councilmen's meals

idle to worthless compared to

divine secret ... spirits Subtle refers to the belief of some alchemists that their knowledge was spiritual in nature, and had originated in the far East

tradition Ananias rises to the bait when Subtle uses this word; traditions, and hence customs and rites, were seen as popish by Puritans who kept to a strictly literal interpretation of the words of the Bible

competent sufficient

gi' it you in exchange it

expect wait

second ... ninth Ananias sees the names of the days and the months as being Roman, hence, popish

hundred marks something over sixty pounds; the goods will be worth six million once transmuted – a fabulous sum for the time

Unladed unloaded

draught i.e. the latest instalment

tincture chemical solution

> **bide the third examination** repeatedly pass tests for forgery
> **parcels** the items of Mammon's goods

SCENE 3   **Face has encountered a Spanish nobleman who is keen to meet Dol**

Face returns, complaining that Surly has not kept the appointment made at II.3.288–90, but that he has met a Spanish nobleman who is keen to enjoy Dol's charms. The Anabaptists are elsewhere on the premises, making a pleasing valuation of Mammon's goods, which Face suggests could be sold twice over; Drugger could be persuaded to buy them 'To furnish household' if he felt he had the opportunity of winning the widow Pliant. Dapper knocks and Face instructs Dol to put on her Queen of Fairy costume and Subtle his conjurer's robes of I.2.

> Face is seen here at his most brilliant and also at his most confident, but his self-assurance also blinds him to any dangers. He does not conceive that he could be outwitted, and so it does not occur to him that the circumstances in which, while Surly failed to keep his appointment, he did happen to encounter an extravagantly attired Spanish nobleman, might be a little suspicious. Face's exuberance and joy in his own abilities are an obstacle to cooler reflection and scheming. His suggestion that Mammon's kitchenware could be sold to both the Anabaptists and to Drugger is so clever it verges on the flashy, and Subtle can only stand back and admire (line 59). Face is a superb improviser, but that gift and quality is also his weakness against slower but steadier opponents such as Surly. At the same time as he begins to over-reach himself, Face evokes the spirit of Act I, Scene 1: 'the few … against a world, Dol' (lines 34–5). Dol herself offers no objection to being given to the 'Spanish nobleman', and thereby shows herself in her true colours as an unparticular London whore.

> **cheater** Surly has not kept his appointment made earlier
> **quit him** given up on him
> **for his conscience** because he is a Protestant, and is therefore keeping 'private', and not associating with other Spaniards; but he is characterised by Spanish costume and Spanish gold

munition provisions

round trunks breeches reaching down to the knees; sometimes stuffed to increase their apparent size

bath brothels often did business under cover of being bathhouses

colour pretext

battery assault

doxy 'tart'

Adalantado Spanish nobleman

in bank i.e. safely put away

against he ha' in anticipation of winning over

circle the 'round' of line 2 is here reinterpreted as a magician's circle

tune your virginal get ready to perform

SCENE 4   **Dapper returns. Drugger brings Kastril, and Face is attracted by the apparent promise of Kastril's available sister**

Dapper returns but is interrupted by the arrival of Drugger with his acquaintance Kastril. Kastril has seen 'the angry boys', fashionable swaggerers, taking tobacco in Drugger's shop and he himself wishes to be initiated into all the modish styles of fashion, quarrelling and living on one's wits, skills that Kastril believes Subtle can provide, and which Face confirms he can. He also tells Kastril that another of Subtle's skills is 'making matches, for young widows' (line 101), at which Kastril resolves to rush off to bring his own sister. Face confirms that Dapper has performed all of the humiliating ceremonies that were specified at the end of I.2, and that he has brought more money.

> There are signs that the schemers might be starting to over-reach themselves again; two previous 'gulls', Dapper and Drugger, return with their varying requirements, and a new one, Kastril, appears bringing with him the promise of his accessible sister. Face already seems to be thinking beyond the readily available attractions of Dol. His inquiry at line 11, 'Where's the widow?', is too abrupt and eager, and later in the scene he has an ominous aside: 'Subtle and I / Must wrestle for her' (lines 133–4). We think of his lowly situation and his poverty as described in the

first scene of the play; a rich widow would be a spectacular catch for a man such as Face, and in his desire to secure this prize he may be about to overlook the scrupulous attention to detail that is required to manage all the other concurrent swindles that he has going. He speaks fluently and with a sense of easy enjoyment of his own ability to Kastril, but is not alert enough to Kastril's truculence, as evinced in his aggressive short lines and constant questioning.

her Highness the Queen of Fairy

aunt as in 'Your aunt of Fairy', I.1.149

damask at Drugger's previous appearance, II.6.72–5, Subtle indicated to Drugger that he should bring not only the agreeable young widow and her brother, but a suit of damask (fine silk) for the Alchemist

'Good time all in good time

sorry else poorer otherwise

carry a business manage, or officiate in, a duel

the least shadow of a hair to the finest degree of detail

instrument instructional document

height on't Face proceeds to explain the elaborate rules of quarrelling and duelling, using terms derived from geometry

mortality mortal danger

give ... by call your opponent a liar, or be called one by him

in oblique an indirect accusation

in circle a roundabout accusation

in diameter a direct accusation

subtlety, but he reads it however complicated it is, he understands it

o' your standing just like you!

spend ruin

vented thrown away

Upmost ... Christmas give him the seat of honour at the gambling tables all through the main gambling season

next his trencher served onto his plate

You shall have suppose you had

with him i.e. with Subtle; Subtle can help even someone who thinks that they are really out of luck

sufficient adequately rich, self-supporting

commodity the 'commodity swindle' as described at II.1.11–14. Face goes on to describe how Subtle is supposedly able to ease a young man through such urban dangers

parcels goods

went off? fell out?

the vinegar, / And the clean shirt as specified at I.2.166–74

But that although

just precise; with the implication, 'painfully penny-pinching'

SCENE 5 **Dapper is being humiliated by the 'Queen of Fairy', when Mammon comes back**

Subtle enters 'disguised as a Priest of Fairy' for the gulling of Dapper, who is blindfolded and subjected to a humiliating cross-dressing routine while being persuaded to divest himself of all his worldly possessions – and the gang help themselves to various coins, pinching him (line 36) in order to extract the last half-crown. Mammon returns, and Dapper is gagged with a piece of gingerbread and stowed in the toilet, 'Fortune's privy lodgings' (line 79).

> The mockery made of Dapper is hilarious but it may also cause the audience some unease: what has Dapper done to deserve this? Yet the comic inventiveness and energy of the swindlers overrides most scruples. The humour is both ingenious and coarse, as in the use of a piece of gingerbread to stop Dapper's mouth; the strong taste may help to overcome Dapper's protests at the vigorous 'fumigation' that he will encounter in the privy. The swindlers' resourcefulness continues to lead them to believe that they can cope with the ever-increasing complications of their situation. They continue to demonstrate their flexibility and versatility by holding a conversation while simultaneously bewitching Dapper with 'fairy talk'. Face continues to demonstrate his resourcefulness when he is helping to organise the disposal of Dapper during the course of the last few lines of this scene; he is simultaneously changing into his 'Lungs' disguise in readiness for Mammon.

her Grace's cousin i.e. Dapper

fasting the instructions as given to Dapper (I.2.165–70)

near intimate

being ... rent a piece was torn off to wrap him in when he was a child

his state his fortune

Directly openly

transitory i.e. material

Ti, ti fairy language! Subtle and Face are pretending to be elves

lay him back i.e. move him back from the fire

till his back be turned the pretence has been that Subtle is ignorant of Mammon's lust for the mad lady (II.3.211–51)

suit Face's 'Lungs' costume

trencher plate

stay your stomach quell your hunger

and 'twere this two hours even if he had to wait for two hours

stay in 's mouth a gag

crinkle recoil

privy lavatory

I am yours over the previous few lines, Face should have been changing into his costume as Lungs

ACT IV

SCENE 1 Mammon arrives to woo Dol

At the end of II.3, Face promised to recommend Mammon to the mad 'lord's sister' (II.3.221), and now he is about to fulfil his promise to introduce him to the lady, reminding him not to mention 'divinity' lest this should trigger another of her mad fits. Mammon praises Dol in extravagant terms, and her responses are very cautious. Face finds the whole scene so funny that he has to retire to give free rein to his laughter (line 63). Mammon's wooing reaches a pitch of fantastical whimsicality. At this point Face returns. He does not want Subtle to hear the noise the courting couple might make, and asks them to retire to another part of the building.

> Mammon's speeches continue his earlier **hyperbole**; he is simultaneously magnificent and laughable. We see a side of Dol that perhaps recalls her common sense rebuking of her partners in

the first scene of the play; she, at least, seems to be aware of the pitfalls of the situation, and is watchful and prudent in her responses to Mammon. Face is maintaining his fiction that the sanctimonious alchemist will be enraged should Mammon appear to compromise his purity by committing acts of bodily uncleanliness with Dol, but this pretend scheming is also an actual deception – he hopes to milk Mammon of some extra funds on the side, and his readiness to work behind Subtle's back also prepares us for his betrayal in Act V.

in her fit mad to
divinity theology; the lady had gone mad with reading too much of this (II.3.238)
controversy religious debate
house family
herald genealogist
antiquary historian
suckle nurse
vesture dress
enlarge advertise
gat begat, fathered
Austriac Austrian, i.e. Hapsburg; the Hapsburgs were noted for their family trait of having large lower lips
costermonger fruit-seller
art artifice
the stepdame i.e. Dol, in her physical perfection, is the only true daughter of Mother Nature
mathematics astrology
distillation chemistry
better appear better
adamant indestructible substance
burning magnifying
monarchy ... Prince referring to the 'kingdom' of I.1, with Subtle as its 'Sovereign' or 'Prince'
mullets fish that were a luxury in Roman times
Rabbins rabbis; theology is not to be discussed in Dol's presence (line 9)

SCENE 2   Face and Subtle both desire Dame Pliant

Kastril and Dame Pliant are arriving, and Face and Subtle hold a terse conversation concerning which of them is to win Dame Pliant. Subtle purports to give Kastril a lesson in quarrelling, before turning his attentions to the lady. Face returns in his 'Captain's' outfit, and also advises Subtle in an aside that the 'Spanish Count' has arrived. Face is obliged to attend to the Spaniard, while Subtle promises to give Kastril further instruction in quarrelling, and to allow Dame Pliant to see her future in his crystal ball.

It has earlier been made apparent that Dame Pliant is going to be a cause of conflict between Face and Subtle ('Subtle, and I / Must wrestle for her', III.4.133–4), and the terse half-lines at the start of this scene suggest the tension between the two men. We are reminded of the quarrel in the first scene of the play; they are both too full of themselves to be truly compatible, and they have both had too rough a time in their lives so far to be able to pass lightly over the opportunity to marry a rich widow.

Subtle has the initiative, as Face savagely confesses: 'You'll ha' the first kiss, 'cause I am not ready' (line 8). Face has to go and change from being 'Lungs' for Mammon to being the man-about-town 'Captain' for Kastril, and that will give Subtle the first opportunity to ingratiate himself with Dame Pliant, an opportunity of which he takes full advantage – his supposed skills in palmistry and phrenology require him to assess the lady by means of close physical contact, and this is a situation which Jonson exploits by means of innuendo; for example, the *monte veneris* to which Subtle refers at line 46 is a term that can be applied to the swelling at the base of the thumb, but it is also used to refer to the female pudendum. Face is temporarily defeated, but it is not in his nature to give in: 'She is a delicate dab-chick! I must have her' (line 60).

suit ... flap Face has to change into his Captain's costume, and wishes it would instantly drop from above, like a theatre curtain; he does not want to depart the stage because that would leave Subtle alone with Dame Pliant

line direction

centre position

I am aforehand I started it

canons principles

predicaments statements

saluted greeted

rivo ... annularis mock phrenology and palmistry, giving Subtle an excuse to examine and feel Pliant

he is no knight i.e. the man I want her to marry

the Count the Spanish Don

fustian worthless

SCENE 3   **Face and Subtle quarrel over who is to claim the widow Pliant. They in their turn are completely deceived by Surly in his Spanish disguise**

The two schemers are quarrelling over Dame Pliant; Face is insistent that he is the one who should have her, but Subtle threatens to betray him to Dol. Face offers some of his profits from their joint operation, but Subtle again threatens to reveal all to Dol. Surly arrives, disguised as a Spanish count. Completely unaware of who he in fact is, Subtle and Face exhibit extreme hilarity at his appearance; Surly is dressed in an exaggeratedly Spanish style of the times with a huge ruff around his neck, and his head looks like a joint of meat upon an elaborate platter. They do not realise that Surly understands every word that they are saying. They believe that the Spanish count has arrived to enjoy the favours of a prostitute and, rather late in the day, they remember that Dol is employed elsewhere with Mammon (lines 50–60). Surly's pronunciation of the Spanish word *vida* (life) leads Face to consider the English word 'widow' and he brilliantly conceives of offering Dame Pliant to the Spanish Count; she is not a virgin, and he himself would be quite prepared to have her in a slightly more soiled condition than she is already. Face and Subtle conclude the scene by arguing again over their individual claims to the widow Dame Pliant.

The liaison between Subtle and Face is now openly antagonistic. Face offers or claims to offer Subtle some of their imagined profits, so long as Subtle will renounce his claims to any share in the widow. It is noticeable that the widow herself has not said 'yes'! Subtle declines the offer. It is at this point that it becomes apparent that

Face is still one ahead of his supposed partner, because he still has, as he hopes, the Dol and Mammon project on hand; indeed, the two are negotiating business somewhere in the house at this moment. Face clearly hits a sore spot when he accuses Subtle of being too old to satisfy the lady sexually (line 10). The relationship between the two becomes cut and thrust, and changes line by line. At lines 63–8, Face conceives of offering the widow to the Spaniard, and Subtle tries to make something of this; he tried to sell his share in the widow earlier, so what is the position now? Face now feels confident that he has the advantage and reminds Subtle that this is a 'venture tripartite', and that Subtle should not be trading – it is all supposedly to be 'common cause' (line 76) or equal shares. He further threatens to 'call' (line 81) Dol, so that she will find out about their dealing concerning the widow. Subtle capitulates but at the end of the scene it is clear that he realises that he has lost his putative claim to the widow to Face and has got nothing in return, and he is therefore all the keener to prostitute the widow to the Spaniard, 'To be revenged on this impetuous Face' (line 103). The relationship between Subtle and Face is not going to be the same again.

This scene is short but crucial, and for reasons besides those described above. The audience recognises Surly in his Spanish costume, but Subtle and Face do not. The masters of disguise and play-acting are themselves being fooled and, additionally, this fooling is being done by the sort of personality by whom they would find it deeply humiliating to be deceived. What is more, Surly is further turning the tables on the tricksters by using their own tool, language. Face and Subtle believe that they are being frightfully clever by insulting Surly to his face, but it is in fact they who are being made to look the fools.

Win her I shall win her

in state with ceremony

I follow you I am aware of what you are up to

Brain of a tailor! referring to Surly's costume; an oath and an exclamation of surprise, and perhaps of admiration

ruff an elaborately pleated collar

trestles i.e. his legs

collar of brawn joint of meat from a pig's neck

wriggled patterned

Fleming ... Egmont's referring to a Flemish rebellion against the Spanish in the Netherlands

fortification the pleats of the ruff resemble a castle wall

squibs explosive shells, rockets

sets the folds in the ruff

but's action apart from his gestures

employed Dol is still engaged with Mammon

stay wait

travelled experienced

punk-master expert in visiting brothels

Mi vida 'my life' – Face hears 'veedo' and it occurs to him to offer Dame Pliant to the Spaniard

credit credibility

doom decision

work her i.e. persuade Dame Pliant to have the Spaniard

I call ... Dol he shouts for Dol, to force Subtle's hand

think of remember

Enthratha ... bathada Subtle mocks the Spanish pronunciation

fubbed cheated

curried ... tawed Subtle uses terms from leather curing to describe the 'flaying' that he thinks Surly is about to receive

SCENE 4   The schemers try to persuade Dame Pliant to take a Spanish lover

Face and Subtle try to persuade the pliable but nonetheless doubting widow that it would be advantageous to her to take a Spanish lover. Kastril is keen that his sister should agree to the proposition. She is persuaded to go to the garden with Surly. Dol is given her cue to throw a fit.

The tension between Subtle and Face continues. Subtle is openly sarcastic to his fellow schemer: 'my scarce worshipful Captain' (line 23). Dame Pliant lives up to her name – her hesitations about taking a Spanish lover are easily overcome.

Kastril's threatened violence to his sister is grimly humorous; he offers to do physically to the widow what other characters do verbally. The reader may wish to query Jonson's attitude towards the women in this play; they are the focus of male desire, but the reader may also feel that they undergo a deal of degradation.

jennet Spanish horse; at the time, often associated with 'riding' in a sexual sense

ruffled petted

chamber reception room

law-French a form of French that was sometimes heard in English courts; Kastril would be impressed by it, but it would be regarded as pedantic jargon by Subtle and Face

use her sexual innuendo

SCENE 5   **Dol's religious frenzy and an apparent explosion from the laboratory succeed in driving Mammon away**

Mammon went off with Dol at the end of IV.1, but Dol is now required for other services so, in order to rid herself of Mammon, she has been instructed to throw her 'religious frenzy', a mishmash of quotations from the Puritan divine Broughton. Mammon is desperate for her to stop, and Face, apparently eager to keep the Dol–Mammon liaison a secret, seems to be equally worried. Subtle appears in his guise as the pious alchemist, and he pretends to be appalled by the seeming immorality that has taken place between Mammon and Dol; this will delay the work, he claims, by at least a month. There is the sound of an explosion from the 'laboratory', and Subtle pretends to faint. This is all a device to rid the schemers of Mammon. They now feign an impending visit from the mad lady's noble brother (II.3.221), come to reclaim her. Mammon must flee. By his lust, he has forsaken all claim to the philosopher's stone. He resolves to make a donation to the Bedlam mental hospital and 'Lungs', ever alert for a profitable opportunity, says that he will send someone to collect the money from him. The conspirators rejoice that one of their main difficulties has been resolved.

There is mutual, and premature, congratulation between Face and Subtle at the end of the scene, but there is nothing joyful about it.

There is a sourness and spite in Subtle's:

> Yes, your young widow, by this time
> Is made a Countess, Face; she's been in travail
> Of a young heir for you. (lines 101–3)

With extravagant and sarcastic courtesy, the two men address each other as 'sir' (lines 103–10).

Alexander's death ... Perdiccas ... Antigonus (etc) it is not necessary to understand Dol's ravings, which are garbled quotations from the works of Broughton, as foreshadowed at II.3.238

My master Face maintains the fiction that Subtle is ignorant, in his pious otherworldliness, of Mammon's desire for Dol

lay allay, or calm, with a sexual pun

What, my son! Subtle discovers Mammon, and pretends to suspect immoral behaviour between him and Dol

crack explosion

in fumo gone up in smoke

Retorts ... boltheads items of alchemical lab equipment

depart Subtle, this life, supposedly; Mammon, the premises

her brother Dol's fictional brother of II.3.221, revived in order to hurry Mammon out of the way

mine own man i.e. my reason has been destroyed

peck a measurement

the nobleman Dol's 'brother'

box at Bedlam the charity box for donations for the hospital for the insane

receive collect; Face still has not finished milking Mammon

in travail of working for

case disguise

prove your virtue test your ability

SCENE 6   **Surly has revealed his true identity to Dame Pliant, and now denounces Subtle and Face**

At the end of IV.4, Surly in his Spanish disguise was sent off with Dame Pliant. He has not seduced her directly, but has rather taken the opportunity to tell her of his true identity and to explain to her that she has almost been the object of villainy, except that he acted in order to preserve her virtue. He now hopes that this will give him an interest in her affections. Surly is still in his Spanish costume and so Subtle, continuing to assume that Surly does not understand him, takes the opportunity to throw a few extra insults, and attempts to pick his pockets. Face appears too, at which point Surly denounces both of them. Face slips away, but Subtle is forced to remain.

> Dame Pliant carries on being pliant, in her meek agreement with Surly. Subtle reveals himself in his true colours; he may have claimed to be a mighty alchemist, but now we see him to be just what he is – another petty criminal, and not a very good one, as he bungles the picking of Surly's pockets. Surly's denunciation of the criminals is full of fine bombast, but lacks their verbal fizz and energy. As the play approaches its denouement, all sorts of pretensions are being punctured.

had I but been had I not been

treat deal

copper ... cheat alleging that Face treats copper to look like gold or silver

casteth figures invents horoscopes

bawds ... midwives ... barren ... green sickness all suggesting that Surly thinks that Subtle specialises in occult solutions for the sexual problems of young women. Green sickness was a form of anaemia thought to affect young women in particular

SCENE 7 **Face enlists Kastril, Drugger and Ananias to help him to force Surly from the premises. Dol brings the news that the master of the house has returned**

Face has used the brief time since he evaded Surly well. He now returns with Kastril, whom we last saw being led off by Subtle at the end of IV.4 for his first quarrelling lesson, and Face is now urging him to put his new skills into practice by confronting this false Don who has come to 'abuse' his sister. Kastril sets to with a will. Drugger reappears and is incited by Face to voice his frustrations with Surly. Ananias enters with the triumphant news that 'Casting of dollars is considered lawful' by the hypocritical brethren, and he is then driven to a pitch of denunciatory zeal by Surly's excessively Catholic and 'idolatrous' attire. This is the last straw for Surly, who flees. Kastril is encouraged to pursue him, and Drugger is sent to hire a Spanish costume if he hopes to have any success with the lady; she is expecting a Spaniard, and Surly had nearly forestalled Drugger's expectations by appearing in such a guise. Face has not forgotten that Kastril had been promised a Spanish count for his sister (IV.4.1–26). Ananias is reassured that 'casting of money' will occur in 'some fitter place', and departs. The tricksters have won a respite and fall back to quarrelling about Dame Pliant, but Dol interrupts them with the news that the master of the house (Lovewit) has returned, and is presently conversing with the neighbours outside. Face orders Subtle and Dol to pack their winnings; he will try to fend off Lovewit for today. He himself will resume his former identity as Jeremy, the butler.

> At the beginning of the play the tricksters had made appointments with their clients, and had carefully laid their plans in advance. Now, the situation is almost out of control and clients are appearing unexpectedly. It is in this sort of improvisatory situation that Face comes into his own. Jonson is laying the ground for Face's final triumph, and Subtle's ignominious departure. At one point, Face actually instructs Subtle to stay alert and to support him: 'Bear up, Subtle' (line 18). This is at the point when he has had the brilliant notion not only of unleashing Kastril on Surly but also of supporting his allegations of Surly's imposture by alleging the imminent arrival of the 'real' Spanish count. Kastril is emboldened to urge Drugger into the fray; a moment of high comedy, this, as the meek tobacconist confronts the outraged and outrageously clad 'Spaniard', and Face is again up to the mark in urging on Kastril and Drugger. The arrival of Ananias is a high point in the play's comedy, as he enters the uproar calmly bidding 'Peace to the household' (line 42). Having enlisted the new arrivals to their cause, it is necessary to clear them from the premises once more and Face, whose brilliant extempore skills are beginning to seem almost routine, has no trouble with Drugger, while Subtle regains some credit in seeing off Ananias. He begins patiently to explain to Face (lines 89–92) what he did, only to be rewarded with an impatient 'I conceive' from Face, and the cocksure assertion that he is too defeatist, and would have given in had Face not helped him out

(lines 93–4). The audience may suspect that Face is heading for a fall, but Jonson is to have further surprises in store. Subtle, in a further attempt to assert his standing, declares that 'Now she is honest, I will stand again' (line 103). He is once more interested in Dame Pliant, he says, now that it is clear that she had not been sullied by Surly; it is Face who has been less particular about the lady's condition (IV.3.66–8). Dol comes in with her sensational news, and Face's reaction is interesting: 'We are undone, and taken' (line 114). This is not an admission of defeat. It is a plain statement of the facts, and he is alert enough to make the best of a bad job. He thinks quickly and clearly, and it is he who gives Subtle and Dol their orders.

had him, presently immediately saw through his deceits

Spanish Count Face is thinking quickly and implies that the real Spanish count, whom Surly has merely been impersonating, is on his way

damned ... pay me for the last three law terms he has been breaking his promise that he would pay me

Amadis ... Quixote characters in European romances; Kastril is thrashing around for foreign names that he hopes will sound insulting

Coxcomb referring to Surly's excessively Spanish hat – 'that lewd hat', line 55; see also II.3.68 – Surly's 'cock's comb' gibe has backfired on him

Zeal ... slops Subtle alleges that Kastril has a puritanical fanaticism against the Spanish style of Surly's trousers

prank it with show off

divers various

take A course follow this up

prevented anticipated

brokerly nit-picking

damask Drugger has finally turned up with the silk; and is promptly dispatched for a Spanish costume

Hieronymo's ... serve a reference to an Elizabethan play, *The Spanish Tragedy*; it is quite likely that Jonson played Hieronymo himself, and therefore is sharing a literary joke with the audience – Drugger is told, 'Get your hands on any old pseudo-Spanish rubbish you can'

whispered with him i.e. Ananias

conceive understand

rascal i.e. Surly

damask the silk that Drugger brought, line 67

the Count now that Surly has been dispatched, Face plans to assume his place in Dame Pliant's affections

honest i.e. she was not ravished by Surly

I will stand I'm in the marriage stakes again (with a sexual innuendo). At IV.3.87, Subtle had renounced all interest in the widow, and had shaken hands with Face that this was to be the agreement between them

one a week i.e. of the plague

liberties ... the walls another disagreement. Subtle says that Face told him that Lovewit would not return while there was still a minor incidence of mortality in the general London area; Face claims that he meant a much smaller area – that strictly within 'the walls' of the City of London – thus one likely to be plague-free the more quickly, and so Lovewit's reappearance is explicable

share divide the spoils

keep stay in

shave ... trim both words had a secondary meaning of 'cheat'

ACT V

SCENE 1   Lovewit returns and questions the neighbours about what has been happening at his house

Lovewit quizzes the neighbours as to what has been going on during his absence and they report that the house has received many visitors. The neighbours have heard strange noises at night. Jeremy the butler has not been seen. Lovewit resolves that the door should be forced open.

Suddenly the closed 'republic' of the three schemers is being invaded by the world; Lovewit is outside with 'forty o' the neighbours' (IV.7.112). In the excited chatter of the people, we receive a strong impression of the lively streetlife of the crowded neighbourhood of Blackfriars in 1610. Lovewit is calm and urbane, and rather than being alarmed by his neighbours' reports, prefers to amuse himself in speculating as to what sort of saucy business it could be that Jeremy has been operating in his absence. Lovewit's crucial line, and the one that anticipates his imminent conduct, is: 'I love a teeming wit, as I love my nourishment' (line 16). He, as his name suggests, loves wit, style and ingenuity, and that will incline him to Face's cause.

banners ... claws i.e. as if he was advertising a freak show
Friar ... great thing there must be obscene puppet shows to attract all these people
courser horse
covering having sex (of animals)
made away murdered
downward from below

SCENE 2   **Lovewit asks Face what has been going on during his absence**

Lovewit has been persuaded to knock again rather than to break down the door, and this time it is answered by the clean-shaven Jeremy the butler; Face has removed his 'Captain's' beard. Face says that he has kept the house locked up securely because it has been 'visited' by the plague. Lovewit repeats what the neighbours have told him, but Face keeps to his version of events. The neighbours begin to doubt their own testimony, given Jeremy's reputation as an 'honest fellow' (line 38). Surly and Mammon arrive.

Lovewit's readiness to take Jeremy's cause is noticeable, as is the reputation that Jeremy has in the neighbourhood. We may conjecture that Jeremy / Face has been living a double existence for some while; he appears 'honest' to the neighbours, but Lovewit was not slow in the previous scene to speculate on a potential for naughtiness on Face's part. Face's final two lines in this scene can not be taken seriously; they are tongue-in-cheek, and perhaps **parodic** of the tragic villain in a different sort of play. We have already seen Face slip out of situations just as bad as this one promises to be. The tenor of the play has not been suggestive of retribution.

visited i.e. by the plague
kept the buttery kept the pantry free of rodents

burnt ... tar fumigation
They did pass ... walls they must have been spirits
black pot through the bottom of their beer mugs; they have been drinking

SCENE 3   **Face can no longer maintain his pretence; he offers Lovewit Dame Pliant in return for Lovewit's forgiveness and protection**

Surly and Mammon demand admittance to the house, but Lovewit, supported by Face's indignant rebuttals, does not seem overly inclined to indulge them. Kastril appears in search of his sister, followed by the Anabaptists; Ananias addresses Lovewit as 'Satan' for attempting to hinder his 'zeal'. Face alleges a mass outbreak of insanity and drunkenness. The neighbours claim that some of the people presently appearing are the visitors who came when the house was supposedly locked up. At this crucial point Dapper, whom the audience and even Face have long forgotten in the pace of the unfolding events, cries out from the privy where he has been awaiting the Queen of Fairy. This is more than even Face can handle, and he throws himself on Lovewit's mercy. Face explains that the house was never visited by the plague, and that he can sweeten the pill for Lovewit by offering him a wealthy young widow; the only trouble to which Lovewit need go is to dress up as a Spaniard!

> Brazening it out has served Face well so far. It is even possible that he could have coped with Dapper's outcry (his 'Illusions, some spirit o' the air' at line 66 suggests that he was going to try), but Subtle speaks out also, and it is all too obvious to everyone that there is a complicated situation within the house as well as outside. Face's comment about Subtle (line 71) is quite savage. Lovewit admits to being an 'indulgent master' (line 77), to which Face responds: 'you were wont to affect mirth, and wit' (line 80); the two seem positively eager to side with each other, and so Lovewit is happy when Face recommends the young widow. Lovewit asks if he might see her, but raises no actual objection. Face's behaviour is simple, cynical and expedient; he will form a new league, this time with his master, to replace the previous 'venture tripartite'. Smoothly and easily he switches allegiance. Just as Dol was to be a

bribe to secure Mammon, so Face will use Dame Pliant to buy peace with Lovewit.

wedges ingots

What mean you Surly and Mammon do not recognise the clean-shaven Jeremy

a new Face? Surly has not recognised him, but thinks he must be a similar rogue

fat ... gentleman Mammon and Surly

sister in other words, a fellow Puritan

SCENE 4   **Dapper is introduced to the 'Queen of Fairy'. The conspirators apprise their gains, but Face reveals his alliance with Lovewit; Subtle and Dol have nothing, and must flee. They curse him**

Dol appears to Dapper as the Queen of Fairy. Drugger appears with the Spanish suit, hoping thereby to obtain the widow. He is sent to fetch a parson. Face commandeers the suit, which Subtle interprets as another attempt to gain the widow for himself. Subtle proposes to Dol that they leave with the booty and not keep the appointment with Face that was arranged in IV.7. Face catches Dol and Subtle kissing. He reassures them that their schemes are still running well. Dol and Subtle remain convinced that it is Face's intention to claim the widow, and Subtle urges Dol to fleece the widow of all the property she can. The three tricksters go through their winnings; there have been many profitable operations that have not previously been mentioned in the text. Face confronts Dol and Subtle with the knowledge that he has confessed all to Lovewit. The best Face can do for them is to help them over the back wall. They depart, cursing him.

> Face now resembles the clean-shaven Jeremy rather than the bearded Captain, but Dapper is blindfolded and so does not realise this. Face has returned to report that he has kept Lovewit at bay: 'I have been fain to say, the house is haunted / With spirits, to keep churl back' (lines 10–11). It is possible to read Subtle's 'Why then triumph, and sing / Of Face so famous, the precious king / Of present wits' (lines 12–14) as being sarcastic, but it is more likely to be an explosion of relief. He admits to fear; he 'dwindled' when he

heard the hubbub outside the door, but he is still prepared to scheme against Face. He and Dol put on a surprisingly gracious and gentle double act for the final humiliation of Dapper. In the fast-paced cynicism of the play, Dapper's reaction is a unique moment of sweetness: 'I cannot speak, for joy' (line 33).

Face is now the one issuing the orders, which he does rapidly and efficiently at lines 62–5. His reference to 'queen' Dol at line 65 can be seen as mocking, given his new betrayal of the 'sovereign' state of I.1. Face is now setting the agenda, and there is something sadly inadequate about Subtle's attempts to outwit him in his plans to fail to observe their rendezvous. He confidently advises Face that 'The chaplain awaits you' (line 99) while having no idea what it is that is really going on. Face mockingly gets the others to help him apprise the goods, knowing full well that he is about to betray them quite pitilessly. He sneers, not unpleasantly or gloatingly but triumphantly at Subtle, in calling him 'Doctor' and in asking what good was Subtle's casting of figures (horoscopes, line 128). Face claims to be 'sorry for' Dol, but it is hard to tell whether this is genuine pity or regret at the inconvenience of being deprived of Dol's sexual availability. It is a superb about-turn; two of the three tricksters have themselves become victims. They have been put in the same position as Dapper and their other helpless gulls. Both Dol and Face splutter ineffectually at the end of the scene; Face, confident in victory, offers letters of recommendation to assist them in their future careers.

fume of the privy!
stay settle
suit request
right proper
blood you come on your family
frume'ty wheat boiled in milk
whenas ... done it because your 'aunt' has made you rich
be true to us do not forget our share
if but ... stirring even if there was only a total of £3000 on the table
comely appropriately
forty mark see I.2.51

writings legal documents

spend earn

fit him give him an apt punishment

o'erweening arrogant

pluck his bird in revenge against Face, Dol is going to leave his woman (Dame Pliant) penniless

stock-affairs business matters

jewel they go on to mention other dealings that we have not witnessed

save protect

flock-bed, and the buttery i.e. by night and day

SCENE 5   **The master of the house marries Dame Pliant and then wittily dismisses the complaining victims. Jeremy the butler craves the audience's forgiveness**

The gulls are assaulting the door, but Face's main concern is to ascertain that Lovewit has successfully concluded the marriage to Dame Pliant. Lovewit is now free to remove the costume of a Spanish count! Mammon, Surly, Ananias, Tribulation and Kastril continue beating at the door, but the urbane Lovewit advises them that 'a Doctor, and a Captain' (line 36) have been using the house, and he does not know of their whereabouts. This information has been provided by the blameless Jeremy! Lovewit apologetically confesses to having married the widow. Surly should have looked after her better – it is his fault if he left her available for other men to snap up. Mammon attempts to reclaim his goods (the kitchen and other metal implements that he had had delivered to be transmuted into gold), but Lovewit demands legal proof – some sort of certification – that he lost the goods fraudulently; otherwise it is to be considered that he 'did cozen yourself'. The Puritans are swiftly despatched, and Kastril recognises some sort of a kindred spirit in Lovewit, whom he deems to be a 'fine old boy' (line 133). Lovewit tells the audience that he has every reason to be grateful for the 'wit' of his servant, and then hands over to Jeremy to deliver the play's concluding words. Jeremy asks the audience not to condemn him.

In his opportunism and smooth management of the events of the final scene, Lovewit is seen to be a worthy partner for Face. He shows many of the same attributes: the ability to disguise himself by dressing up as the Don to wed Dame Pliant, smooth control in his appropriation of Mammon's goods, acting talent in his portrayal of the honest householder, and wit, as when he innocently asks of Mammon concerning his goods: 'What should they ha' been, sir, turned into gold all?' (line 73). Clearly, he has been swift to grasp the nature of the swindle that has been perpetrated in his house. He also shows the same capacity for harmless comic error, as when he beats away Drugger in the belief that he is another of the Puritan brethren.

Drugger has been washing his face since V.4.96, and has now returned in the expectation of marrying the widow. Because of the peremptory manner of his departure, it is uncertain as to whether or not he ever realises that he has been deceived all along. Dapper certainly never realises that he has been fooled, and has already departed a happy man. Those who do realise that they have been duped, and who have this pointed out to them in no uncertain terms, are those whose veniality has been of a more serious nature, the Puritans and Mammon. Mammon is treated mockingly by Lovewit, who offers him the possibility of recompense if he is prepared to use 'public means', but Mammon has his pride: 'I'll rather lose 'em' (line 71). He tries to regain any scraps of self-respect that he can, and so when Lovewit asks if all the goods were to have been turned into gold, he feigns indifference and ignorance. He retains his delusions though, maintaining that the loss is not his but the 'commonwealth's'; the public will no longer benefit from his proposed good works. The loss that the Anabaptists experience is emphasised by Ananias' reference to the goods 'of the righteous' (line 92). The Anabaptists are greedy, not righteous, and they are punished where it hurts them most, in the pocket.

Surly has not been punished materially, but he too is humbled. He realises that he has 'cheated' himself 'With that same foolish vice of honesty' (line 84), in telling Dame Pliant the truth of the matter in IV.6. Lovewit humiliates him sexually, saying that he 'did nothing' (line 54), 'did' here carrying sexual innuendo, which continues as, with a mixture of witty bragging and deprecating self-portraiture, he says that 'an old harquebuzier, yet, / Could

prime his powder, and give fire, and hit'; Lovewit's ancient 'weapon'
was accurate and quick. It is Face's final triumph that Surly, the one
person who had seen through the deceptions being practised in the
house, and who had confidently expected to have the last word,
should himself end up being outwitted. Surly leaves the house
threatening to hunt down Face and deal with him, as Jeremy trots
alongside, promising his assistance.

At the end of the play, Lovewit, while coming out a winner and
remaining master of the house, concedes the supremacy in wit to
Jeremy, and promises to be ruled by him in anything (line 143).
Lovewit apologises for not behaving as old men are supposed to
behave in plays, but with a young wife, a cellarful of goods, and the
assistance of Face's 'good brain', he feels that he can be permitted
to break the rules of dramatic propriety: 'Stretch age's truth
sometimes' (line 156).

Pander pimp

Rabbi referring to Dol in her fit (IV.5.13)

poesies of the candle things written in candle smoke

choughs ... daws crows and jackdaws, notorious for scavenging and stealing

public means the appropriate legal processes

harken find

Six hundred and ten 1610

Gad in exile the exiled Anabaptists identified themselves with one of the
tribes of Israel

lying for waiting for a good sailing wind

a lady tom wife of a knight

aforehand with capable of dealing with

copy style

dove Pliant

Than her own state in addition to her own estate

hidebound small-minded

candour integrity

a little fell because he was so reliant on Lovewit's indulgence

pelf booty; the 'wealth' of the entertainment the audience have just enjoyed

rests ... guests will remain to entertain you, and new audiences

PART THREE

CRITICAL APPROACHES

CHARACTERISATION

Jonson's earliest stage success, *Every Man in his Humour* (1598), was based on the essentially medieval concept of the 'humours', according to which the emotional and physical disposition of each individual is determined by the proportion of fluids (humours) contained in his body. There were thought to be four such humours: blood, a preponderance of which would result in a sanguine temperament; phlegm, a phlegmatic or sluggish temperament; choler or yellow bile, a bad temper; and melancholy or black bile, a melancholy mood. 'Humours' were sometimes thought of in terms of the four 'conditions', hot, dry, moist and cold, and a man's personality would be dictated by the combination of these, a preponderance of any particular one resulting in a very blinkered personality type. It is a crude and simplistic way of assessing humans, and one with which Jonson did not explicitly proceed beyond his early comedies, but it nonetheless provided him with a useful and flexible blueprint. In plays such as *Volpone* (1605) or *The Alchemist* (1610), Jonson's purpose as a **satirist** was to chastise human folly, and the 'humours' method of characterisation allowed him to isolate certain human traits which he found to be particularly reprehensible and in need of correction, such as avarice or lust; it could be argued that he never abandoned the 'humours' genre but continued to modify it subtly throughout his play-writing career because it served him well in his satiric purpose and gave him license to create grotesques such as Mammon. The 'humours' approach to analysing human beings – presenting people as stereotypes or extremes – may help the reader to understand some of the excessive forms of behaviour that are put on display in *The Alchemist*.

Jonson makes his satirical purpose all the more clear by giving his characters names that are suggestive of the functions they are to perform in the play:

Subtle crafty, wily, not immediately obvious, difficult to analyse, insidious

Face outward appearance, to all appearances; effrontery

Dol Common Dol is the diminutive of Dorothy, as Face addresses her in III.3, but was also a common name for a mistress or prostitute. Common refers to the shared, public nature of Dol's profession

Dapper neat, spruce, trim; small

Drugger one who supplies some sort of narcotic

Lovewit appreciates cleverness and ingenuity. His name is not actually spoken during the play

Epicure Mammon an epicure is a gourmet, or any hedonist. In the New Testament, Mammon is a false god that personifies riches – especially when wealth is equated with corruption

Surly ill-tempered, rude; haughty, arrogant

Tribulation a Puritan name, suggesting spiritual perturbation and striving

Ananias in the Book of Acts in the New Testament, Ananias cheats the Apostles

Kastril as in kestrel, a type of small hawk. He is described as an 'angry boy', a gentleman swaggerer

Dame Pliant easy moulded or swayed, obliging

FACE

The play is titled *The Alchemist*, with obvious reference to Subtle, but the title could as well be applied to Face, given his ability to fashion change in himself and in others. His essential identity remains as elusive as the promise of alchemy itself. Who is he? We meet him as the swaggering Captain Face, his job to strut showily around the 'suburbs', luring customers back to the Blackfriars house. Subtle claims to have 'created' him but, if so, it is only an image that he has made: 'Put thee in words, and fashion' (I.1.72). At the end we see Face as Jeremy the butler, but this again is an identity that has no security. The neighbours know him as an 'honest fellow', but Lovewit is not surprised to find that he has been up to mischief. As he smirkingly speaks the play's final words, how can we be sure that he really is 'Jeremy'? He would appear to have no fixed identity. This is unnerving. His essence, his core, ultimately eludes explanation.

His name suggests his capacity to put on a 'front' or an image of himself that he wishes to project. To Mammon he is 'Lungs', the Alchemist's humble bellows-man, and in the Mammon scenes he is also referred to as 'Puff' and 'Ulen Spiegel'. He is able to transform himself convincingly at very short notice, as with the quick changes he makes at the end of III.5 (on stage) and at the start of IV.2. He changes his manner and language constantly, as with his apparent rage with Subtle in the first Dapper scene, his subservient respect as Lungs towards Mammon, his exchange of alchemical jargon with Subtle, and his personal expressions of violence, as towards Subtle in the first scene of the play, or of desire, as when he determines that he 'must have' Dame Pliant (IV.2.60).

The key to his character is this adaptability, which expresses itself during the course of the play in moments of improvisational genius. Subtle seems to work best to plan and by appointment, as with the Anabaptists, and Face spontaneously. We see this quality in such moments as when he conceives of selling on Mammon's goods – already sold to the Puritans – to Drugger; his instant envisioning of the potential of Kastril and the widow in III.4; his idea to offer Dame Pliant to the 'Spaniard' in place of Dol; his brilliant enlistment of his victims as his allies to confront Surly when Surly attempts to denounce him; or his attempts to hold the fort when Lovewit arrives, with allegations of plaguey cats and mass outbreaks of insanity in the neighbourhood. He is a supreme opportunist who can detect potential in the most unlikely situations; we can surmise that he was doing this even before the start of the play, if we can trust his own account of how he detected the inherent talent of the wretched Subtle at Pie Corner (I.1).

Subtle gives a mocking account of the stratagems Face used to adopt in order to supplement his income. He has, it seems, always been prepared to behave illegally and to defraud his fellow man. As readers or audience, we admire his inventiveness and his lightning wit, but also have to acknowledge that he is not always a very nice person to know. He does not appear to need human emotional contact, and will abandon all thoughts of Dol and of Dame Pliant when it comes to saving himself. There is real venom in some of his exchanges with Subtle, as at the end of I.3. He will drop Dol without a second thought if he feels he has a chance of claiming Dame Pliant – his lust is directed indiscriminately; he does not hesitate to betray Dol and Subtle at the end of the play and to triumph happily over this; and he is always ready to work behind Subtle's back, in spite of Dol's injunctions at the start of the play that they all need each other. He sums up his attitude towards the end of the first scene of the play: 'prove today, who shall shark best'.

Against this we can set some human qualities which show him to be more than just a predatory, grasping creature. His over-confidence and constant impulse to over-reach himself are weaknesses but can result in moments of glorious mischief-making for its own sake, as when he accompanies Surly and Mammon as they exit at the end of the play, promising them his every assistance in capturing the villainous Face; or when he cannot control himself in IV.1 and at the start of IV.2, and has to leave the stage to release his laughter. Above all though, Face is a supremely competitive being; in the dog-eat-dog world of *The Alchemist* he is able to survive where others, such as Subtle, ultimately fail.

SUBTLE

Subtle is the 'Alchemist' of the play's title, but claims to be able to offer many other services, such as fortune telling and necromancy. It is this claim to such a diversity of skills that allows Face to recruit so wide a variety of customers, and so enlarges Jonson's comic scope. We see nothing in the play to indicate that Subtle actually possesses such skills, and Face's description in I.1 of his activities helps to convince us that Subtle is a fraud. There is a sense in which it is possible that he has come to believe in his own publicity; his speech in I.1, in which he claims to have made Face 'a second, in mine own great art' (line 77) does not seem quite knowing and self-aware enough to be taken as being tongue-in-cheek. Subtle's name suggests cunning and arcane skills, but in fact his talents lie elsewhere.

While Face can adopt his manner according to the victim he is currently cozening, Subtle can alter his very language. He dazzles Mammon, and later Ananias, with alchemical jargon, and spouts incantatory nonsense as the 'Priest of Fairy' in III.5. Surly recognises that language is Subtle's chief weapon, and it is language that Surly uses to attack him. It is fair to suggest that while Subtle attempts devious behaviour and to double-cross his partner, he lacks Face's true predatory cunning and is happier on more cerebral grounds. He clearly has a wide knowledge to underpin his linguistic confidence: for example, he is thoroughly conversant with the theological position of the Anabaptists in II.5, and he uses religious terminology accurately. If Face's failing is his over-confidence, his belief that he can handle more than he actually can, then Subtle's is his linguistic energy, which overtakes him and prevents him from a cooler, more rational assessment of the current situation, as when he is so overcome with linguistic mockery of Surly:

> Please you
> *Enthratha* the *chambratha*, worthy Don;
> Where if it please the Fates, in your *bathada*,
> You shall be soaked, and stroked, and tubbed, and rubbed: And scrubbed, and
> fubbed, dear Don, before you go (IV.3.94–98)

that he fails to realise that he has himself been linguistically cozened. He lacks Face's outright contempt for the victims ('stinkards', 'miserable rogue') and instead brings some psychological understanding to them; he picks up on Dapper's unadmitted sexual agenda and waits for the right moment to introduce the 'Queen of Fairy'; he knows that with Mammon he need only make encouraging noises, and Mammon will do the rest for himself; he knows just how far to goad Tribulation without the Anabaptist cracking.

It is the practical details that Subtle cannot cope with. In III.3 Mammon's kitchenware has successfully been sold to the Anabaptists, and Subtle wonders if the material could be sold on again; it is Face who has the grasp of the overall situation, and remembers that Drugger has been urged to think encouragingly of the widow Pliant, and thinks that the goods may be resold to Drugger 'To furnish household', given that the tobacconist is beginning to harbour hopes of marrying the lady. Subtle can only applaud. He is helpless at the end of III.5. He has just brilliantly participated in the linguistic exercise of chatting with Face whilst simultaneously being a wicked elf ('*Ti, ti, ti, ti*, he has more yet', line 34) but cannot cope with the news of Mammon's reappearance. It is Face who arranges the gingerbread gag, and Dol who thinks of where to stow Dapper: 'I' the privy'. Once this is settled, Subtle is at liberty to play with language again: 'I now must show you Fortune's privy lodgings' (line 79). He is not a practical villain, and makes a terrible mess of attempting to pick Surly's pockets. When affairs become really frantic and the skills required are quick-wittedness and improvisation, he loses his nerve: 'Bear up, Subtle' (IV.7.18), and must endure Face's gibe: 'Thou art so down upon the least disaster!' (line 93). In the penultimate scene of the play he is still hoping to outwit Face, but Face is far ahead of him. He aspires to Face's skills and roguery but in the event lacks the aptitude, and beats an ignominious retreat, presumably to become once more the wretch of Pie Corner whom Face eloquently described in the first scene of the play.

DOL COMMON

One of Dol's finest moments occurs in the first scene of the play, and the audience may wish to believe in her assertion of the 'venture tripartite', but after this first scene she does appear to be the definite number three in the partnership. Her role is essentially subservient – she does what Face and Subtle tell her to do – and Jonson is not necessarily to be condemned for his attitude towards Dol, because he is merely reflecting the attitudes of his era. The first scene establishes Dol's intelligence and spirit, but at the same time hints at her true function; she has a lively awareness of the 'cart', the 'marshal' and 'ear-rent', and towards the end of the scene Face and Subtle casually debate which of them is to have her for his 'Dol Particular' that night. She is a prostitute. She has a republican vision of what she and her partners are to achieve, but in her talk of 'republics' she is only drawing attention to herself as a *res publica*, a public thing to be used at anyone's convenience, which is how she proceeds to conduct herself, being happy to retire with Mammon and to confess to being perfectly content to be given to a Spanish nobleman (III.3). She is a crucial part of the proposed scam, but only as a tool. She is used pitilessly by Face and Subtle, who keep her in the dark about their designs on the widow Pliant; if their plans should fall through, then she is likely still to be available for them. She controls herself intelligently when left alone with Mammon, and has one more virtuoso display when she throws her fit in IV.5 but, in the end, is left used and exploited; she must escape over the back fence with Subtle. She had never sensed that Subtle was to be a loser. Face desired her when she was easily available but, when it came to a matter of saving his own skin, he was content to abandon her without compunction. His dismissal of her is brutally cynical; he offers to write her references to 'mistress Amo ... Or madam Caesarean' (V.4.141–2). She has performed brilliantly for him, but Face is careless of this.

SIR EPICURE MAMMON

Mammon is the personification of alchemy; alchemy is the infinite promise of nothing, and Mammon achieves nothing. He lives inside his own head. He is quite possibly satisfied with just thinking about his desires, and could not cope were they to be realised. They are fully visualised, and loaded with sensory excess, but there is nothing actually there. He spins a web of words to ensnare himself. Subtle and Face use language to ensnare their victims, but need do little with Mammon – he has already caught himself in the net of his own self-delusion. His fantasies undergo impossible degrees of refinement; he imagines luxury, and then builds up layers of rarefaction upon what is already impossibly gross. Conceiving impossible debaucheries that would exceed the wildest desires of the most world-weary of sophisticates, he is in fact like a child let loose in a toy-shop.

For all the dreams of material satisfaction, there is something insubstantial about his illusions; they contain images of mirrors and vapour which help to suggest that there is nothing really there. There is a strong sense of voyeurism. Ultimately he is anti-life. He imagines parents prostituting their own daughters to him. He imagines the sexual act purely in terms of quantity, and not in terms of love or creation. His reveries are sterile:

> The swelling unctuous paps
> Of a fat pregnant sow, newly cut off,
> Dressed with an exquisite, and poignant sauce (II.2.83–5)

An image of fecundity is transformed into something horribly abortive.

His pictures of a world free of disease and suffering are appealing until one realises that these notions are all in the cause of self-service. A grateful world is to have the opportunity to pay homage to its benefactor.

When confronted with reality, he reinterprets it in his own terms. He sees Dol and he sees the great lady that he has been told she is, and not the common whore that she actually is. Even when the game is up at the end of the play, he will not admit it, and he reinterprets his deception into a new fantasy: 'I will go mount a turnip cart, and preach / The end of the world' (V.5.81–2). He hereby recovers some of his damaged self-esteem. Lovewit remarks, 'What a great loss in hope have you sustained', but Mammon is nothing daunted: 'Not I. The commonwealth has' (V.5.75–6). He still has an intact image of himself.

SURLY

Surly's name says all that we need to know about him. He is sceptical and mocking of Mammon's alchemical beliefs, and in this sense helps to voice some of the audience's own feelings, but as the audience comes to appreciate the inventive genius of Face and Subtle, Surly can come to appear something of a misery and killjoy – which is precisely the impression that Jonson intends. It ought to be Surly who is standing for some sort of moral rectitude within the debauchery of the context of *The Alchemist*, and yet he turns out to be a completely ineffectual figure. Jonson's message is that one needs energy and vitality to succeed in the depraved world of *The Alchemist*; Surly is too fastidious by far; for example, and unlike Lovewit, he does not take advantage of the widow's sexual compliance – doing so seems to be regarded by Jonson as being ultimately positive and life-affirming.

Surly claims the upper ground as a moral judge, but requires correction himself; it is part of Jonson's purpose to indicate that the preachers may themselves be in need of instruction. He himself is a card-sharper and a swindler:

> You shall no more deal with the hollow die,
> Or the frail card. No more be at charge of keeping
> The livery punk (II.1.9–11)

Even when he enters with his vastly baggy breeches and Ferris-wheel ruff, he is not in himself funny; the humour is generated by Face and Subtle's hilarity and verbal excesses. He says nothing amusing. In reaction to him, even Ananias is allowed to become a comic turn. Jonson ensures that at the end of the play he is fully aware of what has been done to him, and he exits in humiliation still being mocked by Face.

In spite of his unappealing nature, Surly performs a vital function within the overall context of Jonson's comic vision. He is supposedly the high-minded moralist, but this attitude is seen to be a pose as false as any in the play. He desires Dame Pliant as much as do Face and Subtle, but lacks the nerve to impose his desires. Jonson sees something negative and reductive in the person of the moralising sceptic, and thereby forces the readers or audience into the moral conundrum of having to extend their sympathies to the villains.

ANANIAS

Jonson is reported to have experienced difficulties in rubbing along with the puritanical congregations of his own Blackfriars locality, a fact reflected perhaps when Dol speaks spiritedly of: 'A sort of sober, scurvy, precise neighbours' (I.1.164). And he had further reasons for disliking the Puritans, besides those associated with his Catholic tendencies. He saw the Puritans as being, in their own way, as anti-life as Mammon, and he had a further professional grudge against them in that they spoke out vigorously against what they saw as the moral shortcomings of the theatre. Nonetheless, Ananias, a puritanical Anabaptist Deacon, is a superb comic creation, who has a bizarre vigour that is lacking in, say, Surly. He is narrow-minded and dogmatic and a bigot, but the comedy comes from the fact that he cannot repress these urges in himself. Tribulation tells him off at the end of III.1. 'I am sad, my zeal hath so offended' he responds, but that does not prevent him in the following scene from immediately pouncing enthusiastically on such verbal outrages as 'Christmas' and 'bell'. He is the type of youthful zealot who cannot suppress his righteousness. His encounter with the Catholic 'Spaniard' is a high point in comedy: 'They are profane, / Lewd, superstitious, and idolatrous breeches' (IV.7.48–9).

TRIBULATION

There is nothing funny about Tribulation. In early seventeenth century London there were many successful Puritan businessmen; this was a result of their work ethic and their shunning of pleasure. Critics were not slow to point out that this aggrandisement of worldly goods was at odds with their ascetic pronouncements. Puritans built a literal correspondence between this life and the life to come; a man's material worth on earth might be seen to be indicating his spiritual worth in heaven. This could easily be interpreted as a hypocrisy, and this is what Jonson embodies in Tribulation. He is prepared to tolerate any form of illegality, and to justify it if it results in the advancement of the brethren; such advancement is conceived in wholly worldly terms, such as amassing wealth, and even military conquest. Jonson again has his finger on the pulse of the times. Puritans felt that they were elect and therefore above the codes set by the nation state – it is therefore not implausible that Tribulation should harbour his revolutionary schemes. He is as expedient and opportunistic as the swindlers themselves: 'We must bend unto all means' (III.1.11). Whereas Mammon envisages exotic foods and an endless supply of women, Tribulation is concerned solely with amassing coin, and it is by the loss of money that he is punished.

DAPPER

Jonson constructs a gallery of different human foibles and weaknesses in his portrayals of the victims. If Mammon's desires are grandiose, then Dapper's are petty. He wants to achieve success as a gambler, but Subtle astutely detects an underlying desire for success with women also, and can read the inadequacies of his victim so well as to dare the 'Queen of Fairy' subterfuge. He seems scarcely worth the gulling – the 'elves' Subtle and Face extract only a miscellany of coins from him – and seems to be tormented for the sheer pleasure that it brings the tricksters. Some audience members may find that their laughter has an uneasy edge to it – how has Dapper offended? – but the treatment of him is so slapstick and farcical as to disarm most criticism, and Jonson is careful in his final cozening to include nothing too vindictive. Dapper departs a happy man, and his 'I cannot speak, for joy' (V.4.33) can be an oddly moving moment in the theatre.

DRUGGER

Drugger is yet a different species of 'gull'. He is not dishonest. His desires are humdrum in the extreme; he wants advice on such matters as the best way in which to arrange his shelving. His speech is suggestive of his personality:

> And, where my shelves. And, which should be for boxes.
> And, which for pots. I would be glad to thrive, sir (I.3.12–13)

He is hesitant and concerned with domestic matters of boxes and pots. He has a genius for turning up at the wrong time, which can sometimes turn out to be the right time; he wanders innocently into the maelstrom of IV.7, earnestly reciting his accounts, but is also used as Face's unwitting messenger to provide a Spanish suit and a parson. However, alchemy can work its insidious charms on even one so unaware as Drugger, and he begins to entertain shy hopes of claiming Dame Pliant. He is too easy for the likes of Face, and like Dapper he departs unaware of his victimisation. He is not made aware of his shortcomings in the manner of Mammon, Surly and the Anabaptists.

KASTRIL

Kastril suggests yet a further variation on the human capacity for self-deception; he entertains hopes of becoming a gentleman, but it is painfully obvious that he will never become one. He is young and he is wealthy, having just come into his estate, and his image of a gentleman is that of a swaggerer who will pick quarrels and boast in the approved manner, and it is for tutelage in this that he comes to Subtle: 'To carry quarrels, / As gallants do, and manage 'em, by line' (II.6.63–4). He is brilliantly exploited by Face, who unleashes him on Surly. He is truculent and aggressive, and has a fixed idea that his sister should marry a knight. His manner towards Pliant is bullying; he will stoop to threats of physical violence. This is unpleasant, but can be irresistibly funny in the theatre: 'I'll thrust a pin I' your buttocks else' (IV.4.75). Much of his courage is pure bluster, and he is easily deflated by Lovewit at the end of the play.

DAME PLIANT

She is as impressionable and biddable as her name suggests, and is something of a stock character of the times, bringing with her a message of hope for male fantasies: 'A rich young widow ... But nineteen, at the most' (II.6.30–1). Her one real moment comes when she expresses the plucky Englishwoman's loathing for the Spaniard in IV.4, but even then she exposes herself as being intellectually questionable, as she claims to have been hating the Spanish for three years before she was born. Her objections are swiftly and easily overruled by her brother.

LOVEWIT

Although he is absent for the larger part of the play, Lovewit could be described as its presiding spirit, in that his name embodies its ruling essence. In Jonson's time, the word 'wit' connoted more than simply the ability to crack a joke; the word carried suggestions of resourcefulness, quick-wittedness, ingenuity, and pleasure taken for its own sake in outthinking one's opponent. He is portrayed by Face in the first scene of the play as being overly cautious about the plague, someone who will carefully signal his arrival well in advance, and who is happy to be pottering around his 'hop-yards'. When we actually meet him, his arrival is completely unexpected, and he is by no means a countryman who is out of his depth in the city; he is urbane and composed as he enters upon the disorderly scene at his house. He perhaps knows Jeremy better than Jeremy knows him, in that he is not surprised that there has been some questionable conduct practised in his house.

He accepts the world as he finds it, and in this he is suited to come out on top at the end. He does not attempt to impose his own moral code, but instead is happy to strike a bargain with Jeremy. Jeremy has a spare widow on his hands; Lovewit will help him out, if he stands to gain by this. He has no scruples about marrying the widow at a moment's notice, and he displays no qualms of conscience in appropriating Mammon's goods. The normal order is inverted: Lovewit as householder supposedly has the superior status, but the master-servant roles are switched, and Lovewit even pays tribute to Face by referring to him as 'my brain' (V.5.7).

LANGUAGE

Language has an importance in *The Alchemist* that is beyond that of its obvious function in any stage play, that of forming the discourse by which the characters transmit their utterances to the audience. It should always be remembered that Subtle and Face never actually *do* anything; they create nothing, they transform or transmute nothing. They only spin words to create the web that catches their victims. The director Sam Mendes said of his superb 1991–2 Stratford and London production of the play: 'For me *The Alchemist* is about the alchemy of making something out of nothing in an empty room; Face and Subtle creating something out of language itself. I deliberately set it in an empty room with nothing onstage but a table and the three people. It was up to them to make everyone who walks in that room believe it's what they say it is, to create the pictures in the minds of the gulls and in the minds of the audience ...'

Jonson's essential vehicle is **blank verse**, but it is the variations that he employs with this basic device that give the play its unique flavour. Jonson had an acute ear; he must have been abnormally sensitive to the rhythms and inflections of the language of his fellow citizens, and in *The Alchemist* he is able to reproduce the speech of several social strata, and widely differing personalities. Blank verse keeps its prescribed **metre**, but is disrupted and scattered amongst various speakers in the opening violent exchanges between Face and Subtle:

FACE:	Bawd.				
SUBTLE:		Cow-herd.			
FACE:			Conjuror.		
SUBTLE:				Cut-purse.	
FACE:					Witch.
DOL:					O me!

(I.1.107)

Contrast this to the smooth rhythms of Subtle's unctuous discourse on alchemy (II.3.142–76), or to the rhetorical splendour of Mammon's fantasies: 'The beards of barbels, served, instead of salads' (II.2.82), where the alliteration contributes to an overall sensory effect that delights the ear even as Mammon's menus revolt the stomach. Mammon piles up long lists of goods and foods, which contributes to the effect of excess and superabundance in his fantasies. Exquisite poetry is used to express depravity and debauchery. Drugger's rhythms reveal yet another technique, by which language is used to express character and attitude:

> I am a young beginner, and am building
> Of a new shop, and't like your worship: just,
> At corner of a street: (here's the plot on't.)
> And I would know, by art, sir, of your worship,
> Which way I should make my door, by necromancy (I.3.7–11)

Drugger's nervousness comes through clearly in his repetitions, his respectful addresses and his parentheses. These all help to delineate his deference and obsequiousness. Jonson also captures the sententious rhythms of the practised religious sermoniser:

> The only med'cine, for the civil magistrate,
> T'incline him to a feeling of the cause:
> And must be daily used, in the disease (III.1.42–4)

Tribulation's units of meaning – such as they are – tend to fit tidily into the metrical scheme; he is an assured and oily performer, who does not draw attention to himself by breaking the bounds of decorum. The fractured rhythms of Surly's speech indicate his lack of control:

> Of piss, and eggshells, women's terms, man's blood,
> Hair o' the head, burnt clouts, chalk, merds, and clay (II.3.194–5)

In his anger, he cannot pack in the words fast enough. Subtle's smooth response to this is:

> And all these, named
> Intending but one thing: which art our writers
> Used to obscure their art (II.3.198–200)

Here, Subtle openly admits that language is a disguise, a tool to obscure meaning and intention.

Jonson recruits all the speech of London and beyond to his cause: we hear the jargon of the alchemist, the tobacconist, the whore, the lawyer's clerk, combined with Mammon's orotundity and Kastril's country rhythms and inflections. The sheer noise of *The Alchemist* is terrific. Besides the babel of voices noted above, there is the sound of explosions, a constant hammering at the door, and anguished cries from the privy. There are several stand-up rows. In IV.7 Face deliberately incites noise in order to sow confusion; language, as Jonson well knew, could be exploited to hide meaning just as effectively as to express it.

While the subject matter of the play is ostensibly that of alchemy, the idea also functions within the play as a potent metaphor. In a broad sense, alchemy involves the notion of change, and this is seen at all points throughout the play. Face is changed from the menial drudge described by Subtle in I.1 to the strutting Captain Face, and later to Lungs, the wretched bellows-man; Subtle is transformed from the wretched beggar of I.1 into the magisterial 'Doctor', and variously appears as astrologer and necromancer as well as alchemist; Dol is a mad noblewoman and the 'Queen of Fairy'. The victims hope to change themselves: Drugger into a prosperous merchant, Dapper into a big-time gambler, Kastril into a gentleman swaggerer, the Anabaptists into 'temporal lords' and Mammon into a sort of universal Messiah. Such a notion of change is, of course, illusory; just as lead cannot be changed into gold so, Jonson is saying, man's corrupt nature resists improvement. We are reminded in the play of the alchemical belief in the need for moral purity in the man who hopes to attain the philosopher's stone. And while the gulls see their proposed transformations as elevations to something higher, all they are in fact pursuing is more of the same. Their aspirations are wholly material, and they neglect the spiritual aspects of the alchemist's quest for perfection. It is Face and his associates who have found the true secret of how to create gold; they exploit the ignorance and greed of their fellow men.

Subtle speaks of having alchemised Face's very existence, but all he has in fact 'created' is a creature who simply embodies a different form of his existing baseness:

> Given thee thy oaths, thy quarrelling dimensions?
> Thy rules, to cheat at horse-race, cock-pit, cards,
> Dice, or whatever gallant tincture else? (I.1.74–6)

Perhaps the only genuine change we see in the play is the one cheekily suggested at the end of the play, where Lovewit has found an 'elixir' in the person of Dame Pliant, who can bring him riches and renewed youth:

> What a young wife, and a good brain may do:
> Stretch age's truth sometimes, and crack it too (V.5.155–6)

As early as 1671, John Dryden raised the issue of the 'notorious' conclusion to *The Alchemist*: 'Face, after having contrived and carried on the great cozenage of the play, and continued in it without repentance to the last, is not only forgiven by his master, but enriched by his consent, with the spoils of those whom he had cheated.' The play's conclusion continues to generate debate. When Lovewit returns to his house, we might expect retribution to be visited upon the swindlers. But no punishment is meted out. Dol and Subtle gain nothing, but get away with their crimes, and Face earns the gratitude of his master, who assumes his roles as manipulator and would-be husband to Dame Pliant.

The tricksters have robbed their victims, by using deceit and false promises, but the victims themselves have not in fact done anything wrong, and the reader's response is further complicated by the fact that some of them – Drugger and Kastril for example – entertain only very modest hopes. But they are the ones who are punished by the loss of their goods and money, and by public humiliation. In the world of *The Alchemist*, what is punished is stupidity, lack of perception, and slowness of thought; what gets rewarded are qualities such as inventiveness, quick-wittedness and improvisation.

PART FOUR

TEXTUAL ANALYSIS

TEXT **1**   (I.2.8–58)

[*Enter* SUBTLE *in doctor's robes*]

DAPPER: Is this the cunning-man?

FACE:
This is his worship.

DAPPER: Is he a Doctor?

FACE: Yes.

DAPPER:
And ha' you broke with him, Captain?

FACE: Ay.

DAPPER: And how?   10

FACE:
Faith, he does make the matter, sir, so dainty,
I know not what to say –

DAPPER: Not so, good Captain.

FACE:
Would I were fairly rid on't, believe me.

DAPPER:
Nay, now you grieve me, sir. Why should you wish so?
I dare assure you. I'll not be ungrateful.   15

FACE:
I cannot think you will, sir. But the law
Is such a thing – and then, he says, Read's matter
Falling so lately –

DAPPER: Read? He was an ass,
And dealt, sir, with a fool.

FACE: It was a clerk, sir.

DAPPER:
A clerk?

FACE: Nay, hear me, sir, you know the law   20
Better, I think –

DAPPER: I should, sir, and the danger.
You know I showed the statute to you?

FACE: You did so.

DAPPER:
And will I tell, then? By this hand, of flesh,
Would it might never write good court-hand, more,
If I discover. What do you think of me,   25
That I am a *Chiause*?

FACE: What's that?

DAPPER: The Turk was, here –
As one would say, do you think I am a Turk?

FACE:
I'll tell the Doctor so.

DAPPER: Do, good sweet Captain.

FACE:
Come, noble Doctor, 'pray thee, let's prevail,
This is the gentleman, and he is no *Chiause*.   30

SUBTLE:
Captain, I have returned you all my answer.
I would do much, sir, for your love – but this
I neither may, nor can.

FACE: Tut, do not say so.
You deal, now, with a noble fellow, Doctor,
One that will thank you, richly, and he's no *Chiause*:   35
Let that, sir, move you.

SUBTLE: Pray you, forbear –

FACE: He has
Four angels, here –

SUBTLE: You do me wrong, good sir.

FACE:
Doctor, wherein? To tempt you, with these spirits?

SUBTLE:
To tempt my art, and love, sir, to my peril.
'Fore heaven, I scarce can think you are my friend,   40
That so would draw me to apparent danger.

FACE:
I draw you? A horse draw you, and a halter,
You, and your flies together –

DAPPER: Nay, good Captain.

FACE:
That know no difference of men.

SUBTLE: Good words, sir.

FACE:
Good deeds, sir, Doctor Dogs-meat. 'Slight I bring you   45
No cheating Clim o' the Cloughs, or Claribels,
That look as big as five-and-fifty, and flush,
And spit out secrets, like hot custard –

DAPPER: Captain.

FACE:
Nor any melancholic under-scribe,
Shall tell the Vicar: but, a special gentle,   50
That is the heir to forty marks, a year,
Consorts with the small poets of the time,
Is the sole hope of his old grandmother,
That knows the law, and writes you six fair hands,
Is a fine clerk, and has his cyph'ring perfect,   55
Will take his oath, o' the Greek Testament
If need be, in his pocket: and can court
His mistress, out of Ovid.

DAPPER: Nay, dear Captain.

This scene deals with the visit of the first victim or 'gull', a lawyer's clerk named Dapper. Dapper enjoys gambling, and he wants Subtle to raise a spirit that will bring him good fortune. We see that Subtle presents himself as not just an alchemist, but a 'cunning-man' (line 7), someone who is able to demonstrate his skills in all sorts of occult practices. Subtle will have visual impact on stage, having changed into his 'doctor's robes'.

Face exalts him ('His worship', line 9) to induce the necessary respect from Dapper. Face's technique is to claim that the 'Doctor' has scruples about the illegality of the operation; this is simple and masterly, as Dapper, in his eagerness to appease Subtle, is likely to be readier to give: 'I'll not be ungrateful' (line 15). Face too claims to be worried about the law, and cites the case of one Simon Read, who had been in trouble with the authorities in 1608 for supposedly raising spirits. Face reminds Dapper of the parallel (Read 'was a clerk, sir', line 18), and applies false flattery in admiring Dapper's legal knowledge. He is insinuating that Dapper more than anyone should be aware of the legal position in matters such as this, and is forcing him into a position of defensiveness and one in which he is obliged to take on the responsibility for whatever is to happen.

In this scene the conversations between Face and Subtle are obviously staged for the benefit of the eagerly listening Dapper. Face commends Dapper ('a noble fellow', line 34), thereby flattering him, and appears faithfully to relay Dapper's messages, but the little insertion 'richly' (line 35) indicates the real agenda. Nonetheless, Subtle puts on a fine act of indignation at the degrading of his 'art' (line 39) when Face is so apparently indelicate as to mention an actual sum of money. The unscripted double-act is brilliant; Subtle's rejection of the money is Face's cue to launch a furious verbal assault on 'Doctor Dogs-meat' (line 45) while continuing to commend the excellence of the client. In his final speech from this extract he hilariously damns Dapper with faint praise: 'Is the sole hope of his old grandmother' (line 53). In his absurd extolling of the customer's qualities he creates a fantasy Dapper, culminating with his assertion that the lawyer's clerk 'can court / His mistress, out of Ovid' (lines 57–8). Dapper's demurral indicates that Face has touched a nerve, and the way is now open for the introduction of the 'Queen of Fairy'.

The scene is important in introducing us to the adaptability, inventiveness and improvisatory genius that we can expect to see from

Face and Subtle and, in the person of Dapper, to the mixture of cynicism and absurdity that informs Jonson's view of mankind.

TEXT 2   (II.2.34–87)

MAMMON:	For I do mean	
To have a list of wives, and concubines,		35

MAMMON: For I do mean

To have a list of wives, and concubines,   35

Equal with Solomon; who had the stone

Alike, with me: and I will make me, a back

With the elixir, that shall be as tough

As Hercules, to encounter fifty a night.

Th'art sure, thou saw'st it blood?

FACE: Both blood, and spirit, sir.   40

MAMMON:

I will have all my beds, blown up; not stuffed:

Down is too hard. And then, mine oval room,

Filled with such pictures, as Tiberius took

From Elephantis: and dull Aretine

But coldly imitated. Then, my glasses,   45

Cut in more subtle angles, to disperse,

And multiply the figures, as I walk

Naked between my *succubae*. My mists

I'll have of perfume, vapoured 'bout the room,

To lose ourselves in; and my baths, like pits   50

To fall into: from whence, we will come forth,

And roll us dry in gossamer, and roses.

(Is it arrived at ruby?) – Where I spy

A wealthy citizen, or rich lawyer,

Have a sublimed pure wife, unto that fellow   55

I'll send a thousand pound, to be my cuckold.

FACE:

And I shall carry it?

MAMMON: No. I'll ha' no bawds,

But fathers, and mothers. They will do it best.

Best of all others. And, my flatterers

Shall be the pure, and gravest of Divines,   60
That I can get for money. My mere fools,
Eloquent burgesses, and then my poets,
The same that writ so subtly of the fart,
Whom I will entertain, still, for that subject.
The few, that would give out themselves, to be   65
Court, and town stallions, and, eachwhere, belie
Ladies, who are known most innocent, for them;
Those will I beg, to make me eunuchs of:
And they shall fan me with ten ostrich tails
Apiece, made in a plume, to gather wind.   70
We will be brave, Puff, now we ha' the med'cine.
My meat, shall all come in, in Indian shells,
Dishes of agate, set in gold, and studded,
With emeralds, sapphires, hyacinths, and rubies.
The tongues of carps, dormice, and camels' heels,   75
Boiled i' the spirit of Sol, and dissolved pearl,
(Apicius' diet, 'gainst the epilepsy)
And I will eat these broths, with spoons of amber,
Headed with diamant, and carbuncle.
My footboy shall eat pheasants, calvered salmons,   80
Knots, godwits, lampreys: I myself will have
The beards of barbels, served, instead of salads;
Oiled mushrooms; and the swelling unctuous paps
Of a fat pregnant sow, newly cut off,
Dressed with an exquisite, and poignant sauce;   85
For which, I'll say unto my cook, there's gold,
Go forth, and be a knight.

Mammon's visions of his life once he has attained the philosopher's stone are both debauched and fantastic. The 'elixir', he supposes, will fulfil all of his sexual dreams; he will match Solomon, who had seven hundred wives and three hundred concubines, and to keep his harem satisfied he will also have the prowess of Hercules, who according to legend had sex with the fifty daughters of King Thespius in one night. Other men who 'give out themselves, to be / Court, and town, stallions' (lines 65–6) will be neutered!

The speeches are full of excess; nothing will be done by half measures: 'all' his beds will be softer than down; mothers and fathers will make the 'best' panders. Yet a claim such as this shows the absurdity of Mammon's visions and his removal from the normal sphere of human behaviour. Mothers and fathers, he believes, will offer their daughters to him because they know the girls best! In the same way, he will employ religious people to be his flatterers (lines 59–61). He has no conception of human values such as parenthood or religious feeling. His speeches are strongly visual; he can already see these events happening. While he speaks in the future tense for the most part, there is the occasional slip into the present that betrays how actual all this is for him: 'now we ha' the med'cine' (line 71).

In its bloated excess, the extract indicates the true hollowness of Mammon's fantasies. Yet there are other clues within the language that also suggest the essential emptiness of Mammon's desires. There is the sudden descent into direct vulgarity; his poets will be 'The same that writ so subtly of the fart' (line 63), and he proposes to keep them writing on that same subject matter! Perhaps Jonson is crudely suggesting a certain windiness about Mammon; these fantasies are, after all, nothing more than words, hot air. The coarseness is testament to the inherent tawdriness of Mammon's dreams. As he parades naked amongst his mistresses, mirrors will 'multiply the figures' (line 47). There is the suggestion of insubstantiality – the figures will be mere optical illusions. (He seems unaware that the term he uses for mistresses, *succubae*, could also refer to demons that were believed to take on the female form in order to have sex with humans, and was sometimes contemporary slang for a whore.) He imagines clouds of perfume filling the bedroom: 'My mists / I'll have of perfume, vapoured 'bout the room, / To lose ourselves in' (lines 48–50). This last statement is revealing: Mammon is already lost to reality.

Mammon's vision makes it clear to the audience just how insubstantial the dream is that is encouraged by alchemy – as insubstantial and fleeting as alchemy itself.

TEXT 3 (IV.7.27–72)

KASTRIL:

Nay, here's an honest fellow too, that knows him,
And all his tricks. (Make good what I say, Abel,)

This cheater would ha' cozened thee o' the widow.
He owes this honest Drugger, here, seven pound,   30
He has had on him, in two-penny 'orths of tobacco.

DRUGGER:

Yes sir. And he's damned himself, three terms, to pay me.

FACE:

And what does he owe for *lotium*?

DRUGGER: Thirty shillings, sir:
And for six syringes.

SURLY: Hydra of villany!

FACE:

Nay, sir, you must quarrel him out o' the house.

KASTRIL: I will.   35
Sir, if you get not out o' doors, you lie:
And you are a pimp.

SURLY: Why, this is madness, sir,
Not valour in you: I must laugh at this.

KASTRIL:

It is my humour: you are a pimp, and a trig,
And an Amadis de Gaul, or a Don Quixote.   40

DRUGGER:

Or a Knight o' the Curious Coxcomb. Do you see?

                    [*Enter* ANANIAS]

ANANIAS:

Peace to the household.

KASTRIL: I'll keep peace, for no man.

ANANIAS:

Casting of dollars is concluded lawful.

KASTRIL:

Is he the Constable?

SUBTLE: Peace, Ananias.

FACE: No, sir.

KASTRIL:
Then you are an otter, and a shad, a whit,   45
A very tim.

SURLY: You'll hear me, sir?

KASTRIL: I will not.

ANANIAS:
What is the motive?

SURLY: Zeal, in the young gentleman,
Against his Spanish slops –

ANANIAS: They are profane,
Lewd, superstitious, and idolatrous breeches.

SURLY:
New rascals!

KASTRIL: Will you be gone, sir?

ANANIAS: Avoid Satan,   50
Thou art not of the light. That ruff of pride,
About thy neck, betrays thee: and is the same
With that, which the unclean birds, in seventy-seven,
Were seen to prank it with, on divers coasts.
Thou look'st like Antichrist, in that lewd hat.   55

SURLY:
I must give way.

KASTRIL: Be gone, sir.

SURLY: But I'll take
A course with you –

ANANIAS: (Depart, proud Spanish fiend)

SURLY:
Captain, and Doctor –

ANANIAS: Child of perdition.

KASTRIL: Hence, sir.

                                        [*Exit* SURLY]

Did I not quarrel bravely?

FACE: Yes, indeed, sir.

KASTRIL:

Nay, and I give my mind to't, I shall do't.   60

FACE:

O, you must follow, sir, and threaten him tame.
He'll turn again else.

KASTRIL: I'll re-turn him, then.

                                        [*Exit* KASTRIL]

FACE:

Drugger, this rogue prevented us, for thee:
We had determined, that thou shouldst ha' come,
In a Spanish suit, and ha' carried her so; and he   65
A brokerly slave, goes, puts it on himself.
Hast brought the damask?

DRUGGER: Yes sir.

FACE: Thou must borrow,
A Spanish suit. Hast thou no credit with the players?

DRUGGER:

Yes, sir, did you never see me play the fool?

FACE:

I know not, Nab: thou shalt, if I can help it.   70
Hieronymo's old cloak, ruff, and hat will serve,
I'll tell thee more, when thou bring'st 'em.

In this extract the pace of events becomes ever more hectic. Close
examination of a passage such as this reveals Jonson's skill as a writer. The
timing of the revelations in the plot is intricate and immaculately
executed; not a word is wasted.

Surly has suddenly become a dangerous figure, and the quick-thinking Face has recruited Kastril to confront the man whom Face claims has come to compromise his sister's honour. Drugger returns and is also involved in the uproar. The language of each character is clearly adapted to the role each is playing: Face is indignant, Surly makes helpless protestations, and Kastril is loud and violent – Drugger's humble book-keeping in the middle of all this ('Thirty shillings, sir: / And for six syringes', lines 33–4) makes a strong and comic contrast. The characters are strongly and economically delineated and this is true of no-one more than Ananias, whose entry is completely unexpected and is a classic moment of comedy. Chance has aided Face, as Ananias adds to the clamour with his denunciations of Surly's ungodly breeches and 'lewd hat' (line 55).

Throughout a scene of unprecedented noise and confusion, Face keeps his wits. He abruptly silences Subtle when the Alchemist tries to calm Ananias; Face can see that it is in their interests that Surly should have to try to cope with the zealous Puritan. He is thinking ahead. He is aware that he needs a Spanish suit if he is to claim Dame Pliant, and so brilliantly conceives of sending Drugger for one, explaining that Surly had come to spoil the tobacconist's chances of marrying the widow. Even at this moment Jonson incorporates a knowing in-joke that many of his audience would have understood. The Spanish costume that Drugger is to fetch is 'Hieronymo's old cloak, ruff, and hat' (line 71); Hieronymo, a character in Thomas Kyd's play *The Spanish Tragedy*, was a part that Jonson himself had played in the 1590s when he first became involved in the London theatre.

PART FIVE

BACKGROUND

BEN JONSON'S LIFE AND DRAMATIC CAREER

Duellist and poet, bricklayer and court flatterer, aesthete and bon viveur;
Jonson is a fascinating figure. The enigmas that surround the life of
William Shakespeare have attracted more attention, but in its variety and
contradictions Jonson's life is quite as compelling to study.

Jonson was born in London in 1572, a date which makes him
the younger contemporary of Shakespeare (born 1564). His father was
an Anglican priest who died during his mother's pregnancy, and his
mother married again, possibly to a man named Robert Brett, who was a
bricklayer by trade. These details have been interpreted as being
important to Jonson's subsequent development and motivation. He
claimed that his grandfather was a gentleman, that his father lost all the
family property, and that he himself was 'brought up poorly, put to school
… after, taken from it, and put to another craft.' The school was
Westminster, where Jonson established the basis of his considerable
classical education; the craft was bricklaying, and therein lies perhaps the
central contradiction of Jonson's life. He clearly saw himself as an
educated gentleman and much of his ambition to succeed in his literary
career and to impress powerful patrons at court can be explained by the
motivation to leave his humble upbringing behind him. He was to be a
quarrelsome man who was perpetually engaged in disputes and verbal
feuds, and his opponents could always score easy points and hurt him
with references to the bricklaying. The contradictions are still apparent in
The Alchemist, where the vulgar energy of London's streetlife meets
formidable learning.

It was perhaps to escape from the bricklaying that in 1594 he
enrolled for military service in the Netherlands where, he was later to
boast, he killed an opponent in single combat, but his martial career does
not appear to have lasted for long because by the end of 1594 he is
recorded as being back in London and getting married. It is not known
what precipitated this action – he married young for a man of his time –
but his marriage did mean that he compromised the terms of his

bricklaying apprenticeship while having no other trade to fall back on; so it is probably at this time that he entered his new profession of actor, but nothing is known of his earliest theatrical experiences. Like many actors he turned his hand to writing, and like many playwrights some his work was collaborative. This was the case with *The Isle of Dogs*, which he co-wrote with Thomas Nashe. This play was the first instance of Jonson overstepping the bounds of what was permitted. The text does not survive, but it must have contained something libellous as it caused Jonson to spend seven weeks in prison. His first individual success, and one in which Shakespeare acted a role was *Every Man in his Humour*, first performed in 1598. Jonson, typically, quarrelled with a fellow actor, and the quarrel resulted in the other's death. Jonson, howsoever much he was later to claim the incident as an heroic duel, was accused of murder and was sentenced to be hanged. It was however possible for remission – 'benefit of clergy' – to be granted to educated and literate prisoners, and so in the event Jonson escaped, but not without having all of his goods confiscated (perhaps the source of his lifelong financial struggles) and with a second spell in prison. There were further personal misfortunes: his daughter died in 1601; two of his sons died in the plague of 1603; and Jonson and his wife separated, living apart until perhaps 1605.

On his release from prison in 1599 he successfully resumed his theatrical career. *Every Man out of his Humour* was the first salvo in what was styled the War of the Theatres, in which Jonson and fellow dramatists attacked each other by means of their plays. If Jonson was now attracting the ire of his contemporaries, it is a clear indication that he had 'arrived'. Another indication of his status came after the death of Queen Elizabeth I and the accession of King James I in 1603, when Jonson successfully staged an entertainment for James's consort, Queen Anne. This was to launch him on a lengthy and distinguished career as a writer and producer of court entertainments and masques. Queen Anne aspired to match the courtly displays of France, and James enjoyed masques because of his own learning and Latinity, and because they gave him the opportunity to display his own opulent majesty and the physical grace of his court. Masques were elaborate and often extravagant courtly diversions, in which members of the court themselves enacted a short piece, often pseudo-mythological in nature, the purpose of which was usually to glorify James and his wise governance, and to extol the virtues of his queen, court and ministers. Jonson would provide the text, and there would also be music, singing, lavish costumes and impressive stage designs, the latter generally conceived by Inigo Jones. The relationship between Jones and Jonson was turbulent. Over the years, there were disputes over who of them was to assume the overall production responsibility – and hence receive the consequent credit from the monarchy. As can be guessed from the account of his earlier years, this was important to Jonson, and he was not going to relinquish his new status readily. From 1605 until 1613, Jonson provided an annual Twelfth Night masque, and he was not above indulging James's own interests – *The Masque of Queens* (1609), for example, drew upon the King's own 1591 book *Demonology*.

Jonson was versatile. Besides his new role as court writer, he continued all his life to compose a large amount of verse, and he persevered in his career as a playwright. King James became the patron of Shakespeare's theatre company, the Lord Chamberlain's men, which henceforth became known as the King's Men, and it was for this company that Jonson wrote *Sejanus*, a tragedy designed along strictly classical lines. It was not a success. The production provoked the Globe audience to a 'beastly rage', and accusations against the play of 'popery and treason' meant that Jonson had to answer for himself to the Privy Council. *Eastward Ho!* (1605), a collaborative venture, earned him another spell of imprisonment for commenting satirically on King James's Scottish entourage and his lavish distribution of honours to his favourites. Still Jonson could not stay out of trouble. He dined with Robert Catesby, one of the organisers of the Gunpowder Plot, and again had to appear before the Privy Council, this time to persuade them that he was not one of the conspirators. It was characteristic of Jonson to crave royal patronage yet at the same time be unable to stop himself criticising court corruption.

Jonson's powers were now at their peak and over the next ten years he wrote his great comedies: *Volpone* (1605), *Epicoene* (1609), *The Alchemist* (1610) and *Bartholomew Fair* (1614). Not all was unrelieved success: his second tragedy on classical lines, *Catiline* (1611), failed with the popular audience, and at about this time, the last of his legitimate children died. The age looked down on playwrights as being popular entertainers rather than true literary practitioners, but Jonson, with the learning that informed his plays and with the variety of his other bookish activities, saw himself differently and in 1616 he issued his collected *Workes*. He was seen as claiming a distinction that he did not merit, and was derided. Jonson could feel secure though, for that same year King James appointed him poet to the court and awarded him a pension. Jonson's career after 1616 is only a shadow of its former self; he rested safe under royal patronage, and became the literary father figure of his age, collecting honorary degrees from universities and holding court before the 'Sons of Ben', a group of young admirers.

He was still not entirely secure. King James died in 1623, and the flow of royal commissions was less reliable. The new king, Charles I, was the subject of a large number of commendatory verses. Jonson continued writing, but his later works, such as the plays *The Staple of News* (1626) and *The New Inn* (1629) lack the sparkle of those from the first half of his career – although the latter shows a surprising inclination towards a romanticism of the sort at which Jonson used to sneer. A stroke partially paralysed him, and he kept to his bed for the last nine years of his life, although he kept on writing. He died in 1637: his desire for recognition would have been gratified with the large numbers of nobility and gentry who attended his funeral, and by his burial in Westminster Abbey.

BEN JONSON'S THEATRE

The early English theatre did not resemble the theatre to which we are accustomed nowadays. In the Middle Ages, groups of travelling players would perform from carts or from impromptu, makeshift stages set up in market places or inn yards or any other suitable public place. The plays were religious in content, and the players were also all-round entertainers, putting on mimes, juggling, and comedy sketches.

All this changed shortly before the time of William Shakespeare and Ben Jonson with the arrival in London of young men who had been educated at the universities of Oxford and Cambridge and who began to write plays which made use of what they had learned about the classical drama of ancient Greece and Rome. Plays such as Christopher Marlowe's *Tamburlaine the Great* (1587–8) and Thomas Kyd's *The Spanish Tragedy* (1588–9) were unlike anything that had been written in English before.

They were full-length plays on secular subjects, taking their plots from history and legend, and offering a range of characterisation and situation hitherto unattempted in English drama. They were written in blank verse, a freer and more expressive medium than the rigidly rhymed verse of medieval drama, and a form which was to be flexible enough to accommodate the full brilliance of Shakespeare and his successors such as Jonson.

Even more important, though, was the arrival of the theatrical entrepreneur and the professional theatre company. In 1576 James Burbage built the first permanent theatre in London, known simply as 'The Theatre'. Other theatres, the Swan, the Curtain and the Rose, followed. Actors formed themselves into companies, or collectives, under the patronage of a rich or important nobleman or official. In 1594 the best players of the time were divided between two companies, the Lord Chamberlain's Men and the (Lord) Admiral's Men. The Lord Chamberlain was the court official in charge of regulating public entertainments, and his company was assigned to The Theatre, where the principal playwright was Shakespeare; Marlowe's plays were performed by the Admiral's Men at the Rose. It was the Lord Chamberlain's Men who performed Jonson's first major success, *Every Man In His Humour*, at the Curtain Theatre in 1598 – the Curtain, because the lease of the land on which The Theatre stood had expired in April 1597. Burbage had the timbers of The Theatre transported to a site on the South Bank of the Thames, and they were reconstituted as The Globe, which opened in 1599, and where the same company performed Jonson's 'follow-up' to his first success, *Every Man Out Of His Humour*.

With the completion in 1996 of Sam Wanamaker's project to construct in London a replica of The Globe, and with productions now running there, a version of Jonson's earliest theatre can be experienced at first hand. It is very different from the typical modern dramatic experience; the most immediately noticeable difference being that the performances take place in the open air. The form of the late Elizabethan theatre derived from the inn yards and similar spaces in which actors had been accustomed to perform in the past. They were circular wooden buildings with a paved courtyard in the middle – open, obviously, to the sky. A rectangular stage jutted out into the middle of this yard. Some of the audience stood in this yard, or 'pit', to watch the play. They were thus on three sides of the stage, close up to it and on a level with it. They were known as 'groundlings'. They paid only a penny to get in, but for wealthier spectators there were benches in three covered tiers or galleries that extended round most of the auditorium and which overlooked the pit and the stage. These spectators were protected from the weather.

The stage itself was partially covered by a roof or canopy that projected from the wall at the rear of the stage and was supported by two posts at the front. This protected the stage and the performers from the weather, and it also housed winches and other machinery for stage effects. On either side at the back of the stage there was a door, leading back to the dressing rooms, and it was by means of these doors that actors entered and left the stage. Between the two doors was a small alcove or recess ('discovery space') which was curtained off. There may also have been a small walk-space above the discovery space for use as battlements or balcony. Trapdoors in the floor of the stage made possible a further variety of effects. There was little in the way of scenery or props; the stage was bare. Costumes were vital for indicating status; an extravagant costume was a very expensive item, and would form a major part of a company's stock. The parts of girls and women were played by boys.

Even allowing for all these changes in which he was involved, Jonson stands at the heart of another profound shift in English theatrical history. In 1608, Shakespeare's company (known since the accession of James I in 1603 as the King's Men) secured the Blackfriars Theatre, and a grasp of the implications of this acquisition is vital to understanding the circumstances in which *The Alchemist* was written and performed.

It may be difficult for the modern audience and reader to appreciate just how radical and vital the Blackfriars was to the development of the English theatre. It was, essentially, a modern theatre. It was rectangular and, crucially, roofed, holding perhaps 700 audience members, with seats for all of them, and facilities for relatively sophisticated special effects. As in a modern theatre, the more an audience member paid, the closer he was to the action on stage – at the Globe the audience member paid less to be right next to the stage, if he did not mind the mud and rain and having to stand. Lighting at the Blackfriars – in the outdoor theatres it had not previously been necessary – was by means of candles. Crucially, there was a shift in the audience profile. It cost sixpence to enter the Blackfriars, which put this theatre out of the economic range of the

London working class. The Blackfriars audience was moneyed, stemmed from an exclusive area of the city of London, and was very self-aware. The theatre was located close to the Inns of Court, London's legal heartland. Jonson's first intention was to open *The Alchemist*, performed by the King's Men, at the Blackfriars in the summer of 1610, but he was frustrated by an outbreak of the plague that resulted in the temporary closure of the London theatres, and so the play premiered in Oxford, and was only shown at its intended venue later in the year. It is no accident that the first 'customer' to present himself at Lovewit's house is Dapper, a 'lawyer's clerk' and therefore a habitué of Blackfriars. Jonson is putting on, in Blackfriars, a play about the people of Blackfriars. It is a very knowing and modern theatrical device.

CLASSICISM AND SATIRE

The Renaissance brought about a great revival of classical learning in Europe, and the classical Greek and Latin authors had no more earnest a devotee than Jonson, who was formidably well read in them. He admired the control and restraint in a Latin poet such as Horace, and the disciplined structures of a playwright such as Plautus. This led him to criticise the unlikely events and what he saw as being the unnatural characterisation in contemporary plays such as Shakespeare's late comedies. Inspired by his reading of the classics, Jonson felt that comedy should have a serious purpose; virtue should be encouraged and vice punished. It can be seen that this is not strictly the case with *The Alchemist*, but Jonson allowed himself a wider brief, which was the exposure of greed and folly. He deplored the romantic tendencies of writers such as Shakespeare, and believed that comedy should derive its characters and energy from the life observed around the writer. He believed in the 'Unities'; contemporary misreadings of the Greek philosopher Aristotle, whose 'Poetics' discussed drama, led writers to believe that Aristotle had stated that the action of a play must be confined to one situation, and be encompassed within the span of twenty-four hours. Jonson follows these strictures in *The Alchemist*; indeed it is possible to construct a time-scheme for the play in which the whole frantic action is compressed within six hours.

PART SIX

CRITICAL HISTORY & BROADER PERSPECTIVES

MAJOR CRITICS

Jonson has suffered from being in Shakespeare's shadow, but he has had many supporters. *The Alchemist's* most notable early critic was a distinguished one, the poet John Dryden, who observed (1671) the moral difficulties that faced the audience at the end of the play. Elsewhere, Dryden noted the emotional hardness of Jonson's plays generally, and concluded: 'I admire him, but I love Shakespeare.' The play's popularity in the eighteenth century was reflected in an increase of critical attention. John Upton (1749) admired the play's explosive opening, and Richard Hurd (1757) commented thoughtfully on Jonson's use of farce for a moral purpose. In the nineteenth century, the poet Coleridge famously wrote: 'I think the *Oedipus Tyrannus*, *The Alchemist*, and *Tom Jones* the three most perfect plots ever planned.' In 1856, Charles Kingsley bizarrely observed: 'Ananias and Tribulation are the best men in the play'. Jonson's status in the twentieth century was established when T.S. Eliot wrote on him, like Dryden commenting on Jonson's 'emotional tone'. He distinguished between the ways in which Shakespeare's characters 'act upon' one another and Jonson's 'fit in' with each other. Modern criticism has paid attention to Jonson's skills as a practical dramatist. In his emotional detachment, he has been compared to the twentieth century German theatre practitioner and experimentalist Brecht.

THEATRICAL HISTORY

Jonson's original intention was to stage *The Alchemist* at the Blackfriars Theatre in the summer of 1610. It is likely that he had a **metatheatrical** purpose in mind – to confront the Blackfriars audience with images of themselves, to equate the theatre with Lovewit's house, and vice versa. As the audience watched the house being taken over for criminal purposes, they would be only too aware that their own houses were standing empty while they sat in the theatre. But an outbreak of the plague resulted in the closing of the London theatres – an event which is echoed in the play – and *The Alchemist* actually opened in Oxford in the autumn of 1610. One Henry Jackson recorded: 'Over these past days, the King's Men have been here. Their acting received very great applause in a full theatre.' The play's popularity continued throughout the seventeenth century, and the portrayal of the Anabaptists often provoked a lively response. The play was, if anything, even more popular in the eighteenth century, and drew the attention of some of that era's most noted theatrical talents: Garrick, Kean, and Cibber. Drugger took on a bizarre independent existence, and starred in specially written farces of his own.

Jonson's abrasiveness sat uneasily with Victorian morality, and his plays were neglected during the nineteenth century, but in the twentieth century renewed critical interest brought about a revival of his work, and there have been notable performances by the likes of Ralph Richardson, Alec Guinness (a noted Drugger), Leo McKern and Ian McKellan. The play's combination of cynicism, farce and pointed comment on material values has ensured its continued life in the latter part of this century. The most distinguished British staging of modern times was the 1991–2 Royal Shakespeare Company production, which placed a lively emphasis on the play's pace and energy.

ALCHEMY

The Greek philosopher Aristotle had taught that all things strove to attain perfection; for example nature formed the perfect metal gold out of other, lesser metals. It is this belief that lies at the heart of alchemy, and of the promise that alchemy seems to hold out to various characters in the play: that they shall be able to transform lead into gold, sickness into health, or mortality into immortality.

Schools of alchemy existed simultaneously in ancient Egypt and China. The main Western tradition of alchemy stemmed from Alexandria in its Hellenistic (or Greek) period at around AD100. After the fall of Rome alchemy disappeared from the West, but was rediscovered via Arabian alchemists in the eleventh and twelfth centuries. Alchemy flourished in the medieval and early Renaissance periods and although by the time of Jonson it had lost much of its credibility, it is worth noting that its ideals persisted. Queen Elizabeth I is reported to have funded alchemical projects, and no less an eighteenth century scientist than the great Isaac Newton researched the subject.

The key to a grasp of alchemy lies in understanding the alchemists' central conviction that gold is the perfect substance. Their belief was that if the art of creating gold from lesser metals could be revealed, then this would be akin to the discovery of how to create perfection, and so would also result in unearthing the secrets of perpetual good health, long life, and even immortality,

It was believed that all substances contained to a greater or lesser degree the four elements – earth, air, fire, and water – combined with the qualities of hot, cold, wet and dry. It was thought that by changing the balance of these elements, one substance could be changed into another. This process was known as *transmutation*. The sixteenth century alchemist Paracelsus tried to replace earth, air, fire and water with sulphur, mercury and salt; hence the frequent mention of these substances that you will find in *The Alchemist,* as for example at II.3.186. There was the conviction that metals behave as people do; they die and are supposedly reborn into a higher state. Metal 'dies' and is resurrected in its pure form as gold:

> Ay, for 'twere absurd
> To think that nature, in the earth, bred gold
> Perfect, I' the instant. Something went before.
> There must be remote matter (II.3.137–40)

When copper is dissolved in nitric acid and then heated dry, it forms a black powder; hence the excited references to 'blackness' in the 'experiments' in *The Alchemist*, such as at II.3.67–9. The copper had died and needed only application of the philosopher's stone to be resurrected as gold. Subtle's long speech at II.3.142–76 may not always be easy to follow, but it suggests much of the above theory.

The 'philosopher's stone', or simply the 'stone', is a frequently occurring term in the play. This was a hypothetical agent, which contained the power to transmute any metal into a higher form. Related to this was the search for the 'elixir of life', or the 'elixir', which would cure disease and lengthen life, as Subtle describes Mammon's visions of doing at I.4.18–29. Other beliefs relating to alchemy concerned the requirement that, as the quest was for perfection, so the recipient of the stone or the elixir also be perfect in themselves; hence the pious front that Subtle presents to Mammon ('he must be *homo frugi,* / A pious, holy, and religious man' – II.2.97–8), and his supposed wrath at Mammon's descents into base behaviour (for example, II.3.4–23). Alchemy also became closely related to astrology, because of the belief that certain heavenly bodies controlled certain metals; so, the sun stood for gold, the moon silver, and Mercury the metal mercury, also known as *quicksilver.* This is what Mammon is referring to at II.1.39.

Alchemy was a complex of beliefs and ideas that involved chemistry, astrology, occultism and magic, with the scope to blend in ideas derived from various religious systems; it is this uncertainty about what alchemy actually is that gives Subtle the opportunity to pose as an omnipotent mage who has the power to satisfy any requirement of his clients.

RELIGION

It can be difficult for the modern reader to understand the importance of religious issues when reading medieval and Renaissance English literature. In the Middle Ages, the Church held a position of power and influence that is comparable to the status of political institutions nowadays. Until the sixteenth century, it was the Roman Catholic Church that had held sway in Western Europe. This dominance was not undisputed. In the 1380s in England there was a movement known as the Lollards, who were inspired by the preacher John Wycliffe. They attacked the moral corruption of the established Church, challenged various established religious practices, and encouraged a return to the basic Christian values of the Bible. In literature an echo of this vigorously critical attitude towards the Church establishment can be detected in the *General Prologue* to Geoffrey Chaucer's *Canterbury Tales* (1387–1400).

Protestantism began in Germany in the early sixteenth century, when the cleric Martin Luther published his *Ninety-Five Theses,* which challenged most of the doctrinal assumptions of the Catholic Church. His ideas spread rapidly throughout Europe, especially Germany,

Scandinavia and Holland. In England the position was complicated by the motives of Henry VIII, who rejected the authority of the Catholic Church for personal reasons, although he continued to uphold the tenets of traditional doctrine, which were enforced even more vigorously under Queen Mary; but Queen Elizabeth I (1558–1603) tolerated a more distinctly Protestant set of beliefs, and the Anglican Church was established during her reign.

The Anglican Church retained many forms of Catholic doctrine and ritual, and this resulted in continued conflict. From the beginnings of Protestantism there had been dissenters who argued for even more radical reforms of church practices than Luther had recommended. These reformers included Zwingli and Calvin in Switzerland in the first half of the sixteenth century. Calvinism took a firm hold in Scotland, which became a firmly Protestant country, as Tribulation notes: 'a learned elder, one of Scotland' (III.2.40). It also took a firm hold in Holland: 'the Hollanders, your friends' (III.2.23). The Anabaptists were a notorious group of dissenters, who attacked not just the Catholic Church but the established Protestant Churches also. Their extremism led to persecution and exile, as documented in the play (for example, II.4.30, III.2.38). Various forms of stern and ascetic Protestantism in England can be grouped together under the general heading of 'Puritanism'.

Jonson himself appears to have been temperamentally scornful of extremism in any form. He was born into an Anglican family, but for the dozen or so years preceding the composition of *The Alchemist*, had been practising the Catholic faith. *The Alchemist* seems to have coincided with his reconversion back to Anglicanism, but it is hard to adduce any direct evidence of this from the play, because Jonson enjoys mocking extremism in all forms. Catholicism, for example, is mocked in the form of Surly's 'Spanish', and his absurd costume. Dame Pliant vigorously upholds the true-born English person's views of the Catholic Spaniard. The Anabaptists condemn themselves. They claim asceticism and extreme purity; Jonson shows that they can be as venial and as grasping as the next man. He also attacks wizardry or, more specifically, those who are gullible enough to believe in it. In the midst of all the confused and confusing clashes of religious belief, many English people continued to place private trust in the ministrations of their local 'cunning-man' (I.2.8) – a term that encompasses a man or woman who claims knowledge of all sorts of skills, including herbalism, occultism, witchcraft, astrology and magic. A survey of Jonson's writing career would reveal a consistent ridicule of the nonsenses of wizardry. In this, as in religion, he was pragmatic and sceptical.

FURTHER READING

This section recommends some of the more recent books that have been published about Ben Jonson; even so, you may need access to a fairly large library in order to obtain some of them.

BIOGRAPHIES

Biographies include Rosalind Miles's *Ben Jonson: His Life and Work* (Routledge, 1986) and David Riggs's *Ben Jonson: A Life* (Harvard, 1989). Some readers have found the latter to be too modernly psychoanalytical of its seventeenth-century subject. Volumes that assess the works within a biographical framework include Anne Barton's *Ben Jonson, Dramatist* (Cambridge, 1984) and, perhaps more readily available, W. David Kay's *Ben Jonson: A Literary Life* (Macmillan, 1995).

Two volumes of essays that focus on Jonson as a theatrical practitioner are Richard Allen Cave's *Ben Jonson* (Macmillan 1991), and *Ben Jonson and Theatre*, edited by Cave, Schafer and Woolland (Routledge, 1999).

CRITICISM

A readily available selection of critical essays and original production reviews can be found in *Ben Jonson: Every Man in his Humour and The Alchemist*, a Macmillan Casebook edited by R.V. Holdsworth.

World events	Author's life	Literature and the arts
c450BC Sicilian philosopher Empedocles publishes *De Natura* in which he puts forward the theory that the four universal elements (humours) are governed by love and discord		
		224BC Roman comic poet Plautus writes Mostellaria, a probable source for *The Alchemist*
1493-1541 Swiss physician Theophrastus Paracelsus applies chemical principles to theories of holistic medicine and earns a reputation as a revolutionary practitioner of alchemy		
1543 Copernicus challenges traditional theories of astronomy and is banished by the Catholic Church		
1570 Elizabeth I excommunicated by the Pope		
	1572 Born in Westminster, London, probably on June 11th	
1582 Outbreak of the Plague in London		
		1587 Christopher Marlowe, *Tamburlaine the Great*
1588 The Spanish Armada defeated		
		1590 Edmund Spenser, *The Faerie Queene* (Books 1-3)
1592 Plague in London closes theatres		**1592** Christopher Marlowe, *Doctor Faustus*

World events	Author's life	Literature and the arts
		1593 Christopher Marlowe dies in a fight at Bull's tavern in Deptford, Kent, aged 29
	1594 Gets married aged 22	
		1595 Michel de Montaigne, *Essais*
1596 London theatres reopen		
	1598 Writes the comedy *Every Man in his Humour,* performed at the Curtain Theatre by his friend William Shakespeare and The King's Men; kills a man in a duel, is imprisoned and narrowly escapes execution	
	1599 Is released from prison; writes *Every Man Out of his Humour*	**1599** The actors Richard Burbage and William Shakespeare start building The Globe Theatre from the timbers of the Shoreditch Playhouse; Burbage's Blackfriars Theatre was probably the location of the first performance of *The Alchemist;* Edmund Spenser dies
	1601 Daughter dies; writes the satires *Cynthia's Revels* and *Poetaster*	**1601** John Marston, *What You Will*
1603 Death of Queen Elizabeth I; accession of James I	**1603** Writes *Sejanus;* two sons die; starts writing masques for the court of King James	
	1604-5 Co-writes and is jailed for the satire *Eastward Ho!*	
1605 Discovery of Guy Fawkes's plot to blow up the Houses of Parliament	**1605** Writes *Volpone*	**1605** Cervantes, *Don Quixote de la Mancha*

World events	Author's life	Literature and the arts
1609 Galileo Galilei constructs first astronomical telescope	**1609-10** Writes *Epicoene*	**1609** Shakespeare becomes part-owner of the new Blackfriars Theatre
	1610 Renounces Catholicism at about this time and writes the comedy **The Alchemist**	
	1611 Writes the tragedy *Catiline*	
1612 Last burning of heretics in England		
		1613 Globe Theatre burns down; reopens 1614
	1614 Writes *Bartholomew Fair*	**1614** John Webster, *The Duchess of Malfi*
	1616 Writes *The Devil is an Ass;* is appointed the poet to the court and receives a pension of £100	**1616** Shakespeare dies on the 23rd April aged 52
1618 Sir Walter Raleigh executed for treason; Thirty Years War begins in *Europe*	**1618** Visits Oxford and is made a Master of Arts; spends the next 9 years in physical and professional decline	
		1622 Birth of French dramatist Molière
1625 King James dies; accession of Charles I	**1625** Writes *The Staple of News*	
	1629 Suffers a stroke; writes *The New Inn*	
	1632 Writes *The Magnetic Lady*	
	1633 Writes *The Tale of a Tub*	
	1637 Dies aged 65 and is buried in Westminster Abbey	

blank verse also known as iambic pentameter. Blank verse is the normal medium for Elizabethan and Jacobean verse drama. In its most basic form it is an unrhymed line of ten syllables in which unstressed and stressed syllables are alternated. It is a flexible dramatic tool owing to its closeness to the rhythms of spoken English. Skilful dramatists such as Shakespeare and Jonson exploited interplay between the strict metrics of the line and these natural rhythms. Some idea of the possible variety can be derived from the 'Language' section

genre this is the term for a type or kind of literature, the three major genres being prose, poetry and drama. At the time Jonson wrote, the genres were seen as fixed entities, each with rules of its own. Jonson, for example, was very careful to follow the dramatic injunction of the 'Unities' (See Classicism and Satire in Part Five: Background). The three major genres may be subdivided. *The Alchemist* is also a comedy and Jonson took a broadly classical interpretation of this sub-genre as being a vehicle to chastise folly and to reward virtue.

hyperbole exaggeration; a common feature of Mammon's speeches

imagery in its simplest form, a word-picture, as with the animal descriptions of the characters in the opening scene of the play

irony saying one thing while you mean another; for example, Face is heavily ironic in his praise of Dapper at I.2.50–8. Irony may not always be so direct and obvious, and the reader or audience must exercise discrimination and judgement to detect the victim of the irony; when, for example, Mammon is extravagantly praising Dol in IV.1, it is not Dol who is the subject of the irony but Mammon, because the audience – and Dol – know her real nature

metatheatre also known as metadrama. Drama that is about drama; or, more generally, drama that draws attention to itself as being an acted fiction. In *The Alchemist*, Jonson implicitly suggests that the audience think of the theatre as being a house in Blackfriars; just like the houses the original 1610 audience had only just left vacant

metre the pattern of stressed and unstressed syllables in a passage of verse

parody an imitation of a work of literature by ridiculing its characteristic features using methods such as exaggeration or the adoption of an inappropriate tone. By extension, characters and their language within a work of literature may be individually ridiculed

pun a play on words: two different meanings are drawn out of a single word

satire satire exhibits or examines faults such as vice or folly, and makes them appear ridiculous or contemptible. Jonson relishes criticising human folly, but has a moral purpose in so doing. In criticising the faults of others, the satirist may open himself to charges of censoriousness or moral superiority

soliloquy a character in a play speaks aloud as if sharing his thoughts with the audience; he is alone on stage, or thinks he is alone. *The Alchemist* is notable for its almost total lack of this device which is so common in the works of other playwrights such as Shakespeare. Jonson is not interested in exploring the inner lives of his characters, as his purpose lies elsewhere. The closest he gets to this device is in quick asides, such as Face's expressions of desire for Dame Pliant in IV.2, which are simply means of indicating the course of the next stage in the plot.

Author of this note

Chris Bailey has a BA in English Language and Literature from Oxford University. He has taught at James Allen's Girls' School in South London, and is presently Head of English and Theatre Studies at Guildford High School.

York Notes Advanced (£3.99 each)

Margaret Atwood
Cat's Eye

Margaret Atwood
The Handmaid's Tale

Jane Austen
Mansfield Park

Jane Austen
Persuasion

Jane Austen
Pride and Prejudice

Alan Bennett
Talking Heads

William Blake
Songs of Innocence and of Experience

Charlotte Brontë
Jane Eyre

Emily Brontë
Wuthering Heights

Angela Carter
Nights at the Circus

Geoffrey Chaucer
The Franklin's Prologue and Tale

Geoffrey Chaucer
The Miller's Prologue and Tale

Geoffrey Chaucer
Prologue To the Canterbury Tales

Geoffrey Chaucer
The Wife of Bath's Prologue and Tale

Samuel Taylor Coleridge
Selected Poems

Joseph Conrad
Heart of Darkness

Daniel Defoe
Moll Flanders

Charles Dickens
Great Expectations

Charles Dickens
Hard Times

Emily Dickinson
Selected Poems

John Donne
Selected Poems

Carol Ann Duffy
Selected Poems

George Eliot
Middlemarch

George Eliot
The Mill on the Floss

T.S. Eliot
Selected Poems

F. Scott Fitzgerald
The Great Gatsby

E.M. Forster
A Passage to India

Brian Friel
Translations

Thomas Hardy
The Mayor of Casterbridge

Thomas Hardy
The Return of the Native

Thomas Hardy
Selected Poems

Thomas Hardy
Tess of the d'Urbervilles

Seamus Heaney
Selected Poems from Opened Ground

Nathaniel Hawthorne
The Scarlet Letter

Kazuo Ishiguro
The Remains of the Day

Ben Jonson
The Alchemist

James Joyce
Dubliners

John Keats
Selected Poems

Christopher Marlowe
Doctor Faustus

Arthur Miller
Death of a Salesman

John Milton
Paradise Lost Books I & II

Toni Morrison
Beloved

Alexander Pope
Rape of the Lock and other poems

William Shakespeare
Antony and Cleopatra

William Shakespeare
As You Like It

William Shakespeare
Hamlet

William Shakespeare
King Lear

William Shakespeare
Measure for Measure

William Shakespeare
The Merchant of Venice

William Shakespeare
A Midsummer Night's Dream

William Shakespeare
Much Ado About Nothing

William Shakespeare
Othello

William Shakespeare
Richard II

William Shakespeare
Romeo and Juliet

William Shakespeare
The Taming of the Shrew

William Shakespeare
The Tempest

William Shakespeare
The Winter's Tale

George Bernard Shaw
Saint Joan

Mary Shelley
Frankenstein

Alice Walker
The Color Purple

Oscar Wilde
The Importance of Being Earnest

Tennessee Williams
A Streetcar Named Desire

John Webster
The Duchess of Malfi

Virginia Woolf
To the Lighthouse

W.B. Yeats
Selected Poems

Future Titles in the York Notes Series

Chinua Achebe
Things Fall Apart

Jane Austen
Emma

Jane Austen
Northanger Abbey

Jane Austen
Sense and Sensibility

Samuel Beckett
Waiting for Godot and
Endgame

Louis de Bernières
Captain Corelli's Mandolin

Charlotte Brontë
Villette

Geoffrey Chaucer
The Merchant's Tale

Geoffrey Chaucer
The Nun's Priest's Tale

Caryl Churchill
Top Girls and *Cloud Nine*

Charles Dickens
Bleak House

T.S. Eliot
The Waste Land

Henry Fielding
Joseph Andrews

Anne Frank
The Diary of Anne Frank

Thomas Hardy
Jude the Obscure

Homer
The Iliad

Homer
The Odyssey

Henrik Ibsen
The Doll's House and *Ghosts*

Ben Jonson
Volpone

James Joyce
*A Portrait of the Artist as a
Young Man*

Philip Larkin
Selected Poems

Aldous Huxley
Brave New World

D.H. Lawrence
Selected Poems

Christopher Marlowe
Edward II

John Milton
Paradise Lost Bks IV & IX

Thomas More
Utopia

George Orwell
Nineteen Eighty-four

Sylvia Plath
Selected Poems

J.B. Priestley
When We Are Married

Jean Rhys
Wide Sargasso Sea

William Shakespeare
As You Like It

William Shakespeare
Coriolanus

William Shakespeare
Henry IV Pt I

Wliiam Shakespeare
Henry IV Part II

William Shakespeare
Henry V

William Shakespeare
Julius Caesar

William Shakespeare
Macbeth

William Shakespeare
Richard III

William Shakespeare
Sonnets

William Shakespeare
Twelfth Night

Tom Stoppard
Arcadia and *Rosencrantz and
Guildenstern are Dead*

Jonathan Swift
*Gulliver's Travels and A Modest
Proposal*

Alfred, Lord Tennyson
Selected Poems

Virgil
The Aeneid

Edith Wharton
Ethan Frome

Jeanette Winterson
*Oranges are Not the Only
Fruit*

Tennessee Williams
Cat on a Hot Tin Roof

Virginia Woolf
Mrs Dalloway

Metaphysical Poets

GCSE and equivalent levels (£3.50 each)

Maya Angelou
I Know Why the Caged Bird Sings

Jane Austen
Pride and Prejudice

Alan Ayckbourn
Absent Friends

Elizabeth Barrett Browning
Selected Poems

Robert Bolt
A Man for All Seasons

Harold Brighouse
Hobson's Choice

Charlotte Brontë
Jane Eyre

Emily Brontë
Wuthering Heights

Shelagh Delaney
A Taste of Honey

Charles Dickens
David Copperfield

Charles Dickens
Great Expectations

Charles Dickens
Hard Times

Charles Dickens
Oliver Twist

Roddy Doyle
Paddy Clarke Ha Ha Ha

George Eliot
Silas Marner

George Eliot
The Mill on the Floss

William Golding
Lord of the Flies

Oliver Goldsmith
She Stoops To Conquer

Willis Hall
The Long and the Short and the Tall

Thomas Hardy
Far from the Madding Crowd

Thomas Hardy
The Mayor of Casterbridge

Thomas Hardy
Tess of the d'Urbervilles

Thomas Hardy
The Withered Arm and other Wessex Tales

L.P. Hartley
The Go-Between

Seamus Heaney
Selected Poems

Susan Hill
I'm the King of the Castle

Barry Hines
A Kestrel for a Knave

Louise Lawrence
Children of the Dust

Harper Lee
To Kill a Mockingbird

Laurie Lee
Cider with Rosie

Arthur Miller
The Crucible

Arthur Miller
A View from the Bridge

Robert O'Brien
Z for Zachariah

Frank O'Connor
My Oedipus Complex and Other Stories

George Orwell
Animal Farm

J.B. Priestley
An Inspector Calls

Willy Russell
Educating Rita

Willy Russell
Our Day Out

J.D. Salinger
The Catcher in the Rye

William Shakespeare
Henry IV Part 1

William Shakespeare
Henry V

William Shakespeare
Julius Caesar

William Shakespeare
Macbeth

William Shakespeare
The Merchant of Venice

William Shakespeare
A Midsummer Night's Dream

William Shakespeare
Much Ado About Nothing

William Shakespeare
Romeo and Juliet

William Shakespeare
The Tempest

William Shakespeare
Twelfth Night

George Bernard Shaw
Pygmalion

Mary Shelley
Frankenstein

R.C. Sherriff
Journey's End

Rukshana Smith
Salt on the Snow

John Steinbeck
Of Mice and Men

Robert Louis Stevenson
Dr Jekyll and Mr Hyde

Jonathan Swift
Gulliver's Travels

Robert Swindells
Daz 4 Zoe

Mildred D. Taylor
Roll of Thunder, Hear My Cry

Mark Twain
Huckleberry Finn

James Watson
Talking in Whispers

William Wordsworth
Selected Poems

A Choice of Poets

Mystery Stories of the Nineteenth Century including The Signalman

Nineteenth Century Short Stories

Poetry of the First World War

Six Women Poets

NOTES

NOTES